# BUILDING *Character* IN YOUNG PEOPLE

Philip St. Romain

A FIREBIRD PRESS BOOK

PELICAN PUBLISHING COMPANY
Gretna 1998

**Library of Congress Cataloging-in-Publication Data**

St. Romain, Philip A.
Building character in young people.

Bibliography: p. 123.
1. Youth — Conduct of life. 1. Title.
BJ1661.S76 1986 649′.7 85-12030
ISBN 0-88289-483-8

Manufactured in the United States of America

Published by Pelican Publishing Company, Inc.
1000 Burmaster Street, Gretna, Louisiana 70053

# Contents

# Preface

I must confess from the outset that there are few original ideas in this book. Adults have been working toward and writing about building character in young people for centuries. Therefore, I acknowledge my indebtedness to my parents, my teachers, and the other adults who helped me to grow. I am grateful, too, for the many writers who helped me to articulate my own understanding of what it means to be a positive role model; a few of my favorites are listed in the Suggested Reading section at the end of this book.

What makes this work unique is probably the way it brings together so many ideas and resources in such a small space. It has been my experience that far too many helpful resources are strung out in leaders' guides, videotapes, and additional audiovisual materials. I have sought to write a comprehensive and compact book that addresses the primary issues surrounding youth development. If I have succeeded, it is because of feedback from my friend and co-worker Shirley Smith and from my wife, Lisa, who is also a guidance counselor and, with me, a parent.

Finally, I would like to thank the many young people I have taught, counseled, and socialized with through the years. They have given much to me; perhaps I can return the favor in this book somehow.

*To my parents,*
*who habilitated eight children of their own*

1

# Our Dependent Youth Culture

During the past five years, I have had the opportunity to coordinate workshops on youth development for both parents and educators. At the beginning of each workshop, I ask participants to take a fantasy trip and imagine that they have the choice of being parents in the 1930s or the 1980s. We then proceed to list the pros and cons of each age, after which participants are asked to make their decision. With rare exceptions, most of them choose to be parents in the 1980s, usually because of the many opportunities and conveniences available.

It is a paradox, however, that despite the best health care, nutrition, housing, and educational opportunities ever made available to a people in history, America's youth between the ages of 15 and 24 show a declining survival rate. Every other age group in our culture shows the opposite because of the tremendous progress that has been made in medical technology over the past three decades. But when we look at youth mortality statistics, we find no evidence of a failure of medical technology. Biological illnesses are not killing our young people—they're killing themselves.

**What's Happening Out There?**

Drunken driving accounts for more deaths among young people than all other causes combined. During the past few years, drunk drivers have caused an average of 25,000 traffic fatalities per year, and young people account for a disproportionately high percentage of these mishaps. Statistics from Mothers Against Drunk Driving and the National Highway Safety Commission show that 44 percent of all nighttime fatal alcohol-related crashes are caused by the 16-to-24 age group—a group that comprises only 22 percent of the total licensed population. On any given Friday or Saturday night after 9 P.M., as many as one out of three drivers on the road is under the influence of some kind of mood-altering chemical—usually alcohol. Most manage to make it home safely; only one in 2,000 will be arrested for DWI. Quite a few run into ditches, telephone poles, and trees. And many smash into cars driven by sober drivers, taking innocent lives and maiming healthy bodies in the process.

However, drunk driving is only one of many problems suffered by young people because of alcohol and drug abuse. Since the mid-1960s, substance abuse in our country has increased at unbelievable rates, including an ever-younger age group each year. Recent surveys from the National Institute on Drug Abuse reveal that about 50 percent of our high school students drink weekly, almost 20 percent smoke marijuana weekly, and 10 percent use other such substances on a regular basis. Almost 15 percent of young people have tried marijuana by the eighth grade; over 95 percent will try alcohol. There are already over 3,000,000 alcoholic young people in our country today, with 300,000 added to their numbers each year. Unfortunately, only a small percentage of them have received rehabilitative counseling.

Where do these young people find alcohol and drugs? Alcohol, of course, is available everywhere. A Louisiana survey found that junior-high-age kids were most likely to get their supply from the home; high school students either used a fake ID, found a store willing to sell to minors, or got older friends to purchase alcohol for them. The same situation presumably exists elsewhere throughout the country.

Illegal drugs are not quite as conspicuous, but they are not hard to come by. Teachers are usually shocked when I ask their sixth graders if they know anyone who smokes pot and half the kids in the class raise their hands. Young kids don't need to look very hard to find marijuana when they already know older kids in their neighborhood who smoke. The supply comes into our neighborhoods via the planes, trucks, and boats of black-market dealers, but most junior and senior high school students never encounter these hardened criminals. Their friends are their pushers, and one of the new symbols of friendship in certain peer circles is the sharing of one's stash. Obviously, trying to break the drug culture's back through law enforcement efforts alone is futile. As long as there is a tremendous demand for drugs, and as long as drugs bring in such incredible sums of money, we can be certain that someone will provide ample supplies for our chemical consumers.

Suicide, the second leading killer of young people, draws many of its victims from the youth drug culture. The severe bouts of anxiety and depression accompanying drug usage were no doubt contributing factors in a large number of the 5,000 or so successful and 80,000 unsuccessful suicide attempts documented during each of the past few years for 15-to-24-year-olds. Needless to say, these young people have lost hope in the possibility of happiness—a further indictment of our age.

Teenage crime is on the upswing, and crime, like suicide, seems to be part of the drug culture; many young people turn to crime to get money for drugs. Homicide is the third leading killer of young people in most states (and second in a few). On a less drastic level, school discipline has been the leading educational concern of both teachers and parents for the past few years. In many schools, we are witnessing increasing amounts of dropping out, expulsions, and absenteeism. Unruly behavior at home, school, and in the larger community has accounted for a tremendous increase in the numbers of young people intervened on by the criminal justice system.

Finally, irresponsible sexual expression robs more young people of their dignity than does any other form of disruptive behavior. Teenagers account for almost 1,000,000 abortions annually, but that does not even begin to measure irresponsible sexual expression that did not result in conception. I have counseled high school students who felt weird because they were still virgins. It's hard to remain committed to the value of waiting when one is young, when the media and other cultural sources flaunt explicit sexuality, and when "everybody's doing it" (or so they say). A 1981 survey published in *Parade* magazine indicated that 43 percent of boys and 31 percent of girls have lost their virginity by the age 16. That's not everybody, but it's quite a few—enough to exert tremendous peer pressure to have sex. Parenting consultant Stephen Glenn brought this matter home at a workshop for educators when he said that one out of five senior high school girls is pregnant at any given time during the school year. Many choose to have abortions, but a growing number are choosing to keep their children, perpetuating the single-parent family system gaining ascendancy in our country.

Alcohol/drug abuse, suicide, crime, and irresponsible sexuality! What's happening to so many of our young people? Why is it that over one-third of our youth are manifesting problems related to dependent personality? Surely there have always been troubled young people, but not in the numbers we see today. And there are, of course, healthy young people still holding their own, but even the strongest find it difficult to hold out forever, given the strength of the peer pressures confronting them daily.

**The Roots of the Problem**

Volumes have been written about how we have gotten ourselves into our present predicament with young people. Educators are quick to blame parents, who in turn blame educators, law enforcement officials, and society in general. Certainly, we all reason, there must be *some* explanation for the changes we have seen among our youth during the past two decades. And there are explanations. But blaming serves no useful function. When it comes to helping young people, we're all in it together. Understanding some of the roots of the problems we are having will be helpful only if it leads us to recognize practices and trends that have hurt young people and, hence, ought to be avoided. It is in that spirit, rather than in a spirit of blaming, that we shall proceed.

*Drug availability*. Since the mid-1960s, marijuana and other illegal drugs have become more readily available to young people than in previous years. While it may be true that the demand for drugs increased availability, there is little doubt that the opposite is true, too. If marijuana had been as available to the teenagers of the '50s, it surely would have been used more. Unfortunately, the social taboos that helped to limit marijuana use broke down in the '60s, when many defiant young people were unable to get a straight answer from scientists concerning the harmfulness of pot. Research today points up several very good reasons why young people should leave marijuana alone, but the damage has already been done in many lives and the black-market economy that came with pot is deeply entrenched.

Furthermore, legal and prescription drugs such as alcohol and Valium are used by more adults than ever and are more available in the home now than in the '50s. The accompanying increase in drug use, abuse, and dependency robs many young people of the emotional discipline they need in order to grow.

*Lack of significant involvement with adults.* In the '30s and '40s, young people spent several hours a day involved in activities that were important to the well-being of the family. Adulthood was no mystery to them; their lives at home and in school prepared them for their adult roles. Today, however, studies reveal that young people spend only about 20 minutes a day communicating with their parents, and only five of these minutes might involve some kind of meaningful exchange; the rest of the time is taken up with reminders, arguing, checking-up, and other unpleasant duties. In many homes, both parents work; in many others, there is only one parent. Both are stressful situations that can put a strain on parent-child relationships.

In addition to little involvement with parents, young people from junior high school on up are shuffled from class to class throughout the school day, seldom developing the kind of rapport with their teachers found in the self-contained classrooms of lower grades. Our institutions of home and school seem to desert young people at about the age of 13—just when peer pressure becomes so intense. (Maybe this is why peer pressure runs rampant.) Lacking significant involvement with adults, young people draw upon rock stars, athletes, and television characters for role models. Today's youths are thus the first generation to form their predominant images of adulthood from an assemblage of unrealistic or fictional characters.

*Television.* Young people today watch an average of six hours of television per day. While the educational and entertainment values of television are as valid today as ever before, we know we pay a price for this pastime. Watching television is a form of passive behavior that cuts into time that could be spent doing healthier activities. The government report *Television and Behavior* indicated clear correlations between aggressive behavior and amounts and types of viewing. Prime-time television characters drink alcohol twice as often as coffee and many times more often than soft drinks or water. Is that a healthy picture to give kids of the real world?

We know, too, that television advertising deeply influences our attitudes; since cigarette advertising was banned from television in the early '70s, smoking among high schoolers has dropped by 50 percent. Television advertising promotes a consumeristic, hedonistic value system and a do-drugs/avoid-pain mentality that plays right into the hands of the drug culture.

Much more could be written about the changes that drug availability, deficient family life, and television have made in the lifestyles of American youth, but it would be pointless to go on. In summary, the problem seems to be their lack of involvement with significant adults and, consequently, their increased reliance on passive forms of entertainment to provide a sense of meaning of life. The result has been dependency to an extent that, I believe, threatens the future of America.

**Profile of a Dependent Youth**

What do we mean when we talk about a dependent person? For my purposes here, I am referring to a person who cannot, using his or her internal resources, adapt to our changing environment in such a manner as to sustain health and spiritual growth. We are all born dependent, but we usually learn through the years how to utilize our own potential to meet life's challenges. If we do not learn this, we will have to be taken care of by society, resort to criminal behavior to secure goods, or perish altogether. This is the situation now confronting millions of our young people.

After years of research by institutions as diverse as mental health associations, alcohol and drug abuse councils, and criminal justice agencies, we now know what characteristics identify a dependent personality. We know, too, that this profile is the same for substance-abusing young people, juvenile delinquents, and kids struggling with sexual pressures. These problems all seem to be manifestations of the same kinds of character deficiencies, although in the case of substance abusers, the drug usage actually creates these deficiencies and so is a primary source of dependency. Dependent youth lack two very important strengths: self-worth and life-coping skills. Let us break these down further.

*Low self-worth.* Dependent young people do not believe they are good and lovable. They feel powerless and insignificant, and they lack a sense of belonging to a healthy, intimate group. Compensating for their loneliness, fear of life, and self-doubt, they often act defiantly and with a false air of independence. Sex seems to be a shortcut to intimacy, but they soon discover that sex without love becomes hollow and self-serving, further deepening their sense of loneliness and alienation. Drugs and alcohol bring temporary relief from emotional pain but cause greater emotional dependency in the long run.

After a while, the self-destructive behaviors that go with low self-worth seem, in the young person's mind and in society's judgment, to validate his internal perceptions of worthlessness. Thus harmful self-fulfilling prophecies gain their place in the minds of many young people: they say to themselves, "I'm no good and I can't do anything right; since I can't do anything right, I'm no good."

*Poor life-coping skills.* By this I mean a lack of clarity about one's values and goals, poor self-discipline and, consequently, irresponsible behavior. Self-discipline is the ability to gear behavior toward identified goals—to sacrifice something now for a higher good later. Getting an education, for example, requires self-discipline, for the benefits will not be completely realized for years. Refusing a beer or a joint because it conflicts with one's values and damages health also requires self-discipline. Establishing healthy friendships and love relationships always demands of us a certain amount of self-sacrifice, for our wants and others' demands often come into conflict. Yet education, health, and relationships are three areas where dependent young people are hurting most. How will they ever experience happiness if they do not learn to develop skills in these areas?

**Questions for Reflection and Discussion**

1. How do you perceive the problems of alcohol and drug availability in your area?
2. What do you believe to be the most serious problems facing young people today?

3. Why do you believe so many young people have dependent personalities?
4. How do the young people you work with feel about alcohol, drugs, and sex?

# 2

# Becoming a Positive Role Model

If the absence of significant involvement with adults has helped to bring about dependency in young people, then it follows that involvement will foster habilitation. This has been my experience and the experience of thousands of other adults who work daily to help build character in young people. Young people are literally starving for attention from adults. Once taken seriously by caring, concerned adults, most begin to grow at surprisingly quick rates. Kids chronically addicted to drugs and alcohol or those whose emotional problems require professional help cannot begin to grow without involvement and direction from adults. The need for a mentor or adult guide seems to be built into the psyches of young people as they go through their years of struggle for identity. We can help to meet that need.

Just because an adult occupies a place of significance in the life of a young person does not guarantee that he or she will be looked up to as a role model, however. Parents, teachers, coaches, and members of the clergy sometimes forget that their privileged roles can be forfeited. We often lament the loss of the full-time homemaker, but I know of many situations where the mother staying at home "for the kids" has such poor involvement with them that they would probably be better off if she worked all day and left them at a day care center. (She would probably be better off for it, too.) On the other hand, there are many single parents and working parents who are wonderfully influential in helping to shape their kids' lives for the better. If an adult is to become a positive role model, one who influences the development of character in young people, she or he will have to offer the two great and essential habilitative gifts: involvement and love.

But what does habilitative involvement specifically entail? And what is love? No one likes to see the fruits of youth dependency, and most adults wish the best for young people. But what are we to do? How do we translate our good intentions into effective behavior? After speaking with and reading the works of adults who have mastered the art of habilitating young people, I have come to note similarities in their involvements and in the quality of care they provide.

**Habilitative Involvement**

Involvement with young people is as essential for an adult's development as it is for a youth's. Yet we have created a culture that is oriented predominantly toward adult fulfillment. Education is justified as preparation for adulthood; Sunday homilies seem more concerned with adults' struggles than with youths'; entertainment diversions in communities are often so neglectful of youth as to leave them almost no alternatives to adult "fun"—bars, nightclubs, riding around in cars, and R-rated movies. We adults, caught up in the security and fascination of our own worlds, often find it difficult to sacrifice time and energy for the sake of the young, the underprivileged, and the elderly. Yet it is precisely this kind of self-sacrifice that prevents us from regressing into selfishness and snobbery.

We need to become involved with young people as much for our own growth as for theirs. We need each other.

Habilitative involvement is much more than occupying space and time together. Many parents and teachers are with young people for long periods of time and never become positive role models to the youths entrusted to them. Then there are those who manage to make a tremendous impact in the lives of young people. What is their secret?

*They love young people,* and this comes across in their attitude. More on this later.

*They engage in activities that require active awareness of the presence of young people and interaction with them.* Whether teaching a class, making cookies, coaching a sport, working with a support group, or even cleaning a house, these adults show interest in and commitment to the activity they're involved in. They are very aware of the presence of the young people and convey a sense that their participation is important.

*They listen to young people and take their perceptions seriously,* even when it is obvious that these perceptions are misguided or based on ignorance. This does not mean that they will not challenge the perceptions of young people; far from it. But even when exchanging ideas, these adults will respect the opinions of young people and avoid putting them down. After all is said and done, this is probably the key to the effectiveness of all forms of therapy, although one doesn't have to be a professional to administer it.

*They discuss matters with young people in such a manner as to help them learn values* and derive meaning from their activities together. They ask open-ended questions: What happened and why? How do you feel about what happened? What would you like to change about the way you responded to that issue?

*They have fun with young people,* even while engaged in serious tasks. We sometimes make adulthood seem like such a gloomy and serious affair that we discourage young people from growing up altogether. One thinks of the attraction of Michael Jackson's Peter Pan fantasies; millions of young people, like Jackson and Peter Pan, do not want to grow up but want to remain children forever. There is no doubt that childhood can be fun and the responsibilities that come with adulthood can be dreary, but this is not the whole story. With growing up comes more freedom, and adults who have learned to use their freedom in a responsible and fun-loving manner can give hope to our youth.

**Toward Habilitation**

Getting a dependent young person back on track involves a process which many helping professionals call habilitation. Rehabilitation assumes that they were once habilitated — or made capable — but fell away. The truth is that many young people undergoing rehabilitative counseling were never habilitated in the first place, and so what we are having to do is teach them skills they should have learned as very small children. These habilitation skills ought to be taught in the home and classroom from infancy onward rather than in substance abuse treatment centers or counseling clinics. That is what I hope to promote through this book.

Before moving on, however, I must emphasize that habilitation is an necessary for "healthy" young people as it is for dependents. We need to strengthen the fragile self-worth that many of our kids are clinging to, and we must continue to help them mature into capable, responsible adults. Adults also suffer from dehabilitative stresses in our culture; habilitative growth is for everyone—old *and* young. It is ludicrous to expect responsible behavior from an adolescent who never learned self-discipline as a child. Ideally, building character in young people begins in the home at a very early age and is complemented by school, church, and community through the years. That this ideal is not always met should not cause us despair, however. People can break with self-destructive behaviors at any age and begin growing toward health, self-acceptance, and responsibility. It happens all the time, and we can help to make it happen.

**Love**

Habilitative involvement with young people is impossible for those who do not love them. I believe that most adults have a lot more love for young people than they give themselves credit for. The problem comes when adults compare themselves with some of the superheroes modeled on television, in the movies, or over the gossip fence. We live in an age of specialization, and I believe many adults mistrust their ability to work with young people because they haven't received "specialized training" in this area. "I can't be like so and so," we lament, "I haven't had the proper training." This is unfortunate, for everyone has something to offer when it comes to helping kids grow up. In the words of Walter Hollins of the U.S. Department of Education, "There are no superheroes when it comes to helping kids; there are only ordinary people who get the job done." And that's what love is all about.

Love is impossible to adequately describe or pin down. The word *love* as used in the English language can refer to anything from enjoying certain foods ("I love cheesecake") to sexual intercourse (making love). For purposes of definition here, I will choose to go with the idea of love proposed by M. Scott Peck in his book *The Road Less Traveled.* Love, writes Peck, is "the will to extend one's self for the purpose of nurturing one's own or another's spiritual growth." This requires commitment to relationships, awareness of human growth patterns, and considerable wisdom. It also takes a warm heart and a few other essentials.

**Love is an attitude that is pro-people and pro-growth.** This attitude is communicated to others in a myriad of ways, and young people pick up on it in short order. They know whether you're for them or against them, so you'd best keep a watch on your attitude and continually take steps to keep your love alive.

**Love offers, but leaves the other free to respond.** We adults can only *offer* our gifts of time, care, expertise, and wisdom to young people; we cannot force them to receive our gifts gratefully. If our gifts are helpful and are offered in receivable ways, chances are that many young people will accept them enthusiastically. Some will not, however, and we must not always blame ourselves when this happens. The oldest story in the world is our refusal of the perfect love of God. If it is that way between humanity and God, then we should not be surprised if our own loving offerings are sometimes rejected. Loving adults learn to offer life-giving alternatives to young people while leaving them free to make their own decisions and experience consequences.

**Love is a commitment to relationships.** This is quite different from the feeling of love, which comes and goes unpredictably. Commitment to relationships means sticking things out in bad times as well as good. People change through time if they are growing, and it is only our commitment to continue relating to one another that keeps us growing together. Many young people are fair-weather friends and bluebird lovers because they have not yet learned the value of commitment. Your commitment to them can help them make a start toward genuine loving relationships.

**Love holds the other accountable for his or her growth.** Love confronts as well as affirms. Because love is pro-growth, a loving adult often finds it necessary to challenge the lethargic and correct the wrong-headed. Loving people believe that life is far too great a gift to squander on destructive behavior patterns. They do not allow fear of lawsuits or rejection to keep them from confronting someone when love calls for it. Love's challenges never attack another's personality, however; instead they focus on how destructive behavior detracts from personal growth.

**Love means you often have to say you're sorry.** Even the best of lovers step on others' toes and make mistakes from time to time. When this happens, forgiveness and reconciliation are needed to keep relationships established and growing. The beneficiary is not so much the person being apologized to as the person doing the apologizing. Saying "I apologize" means that we must get off of our pedestal of perfectionism and join the human race; it means being humble and truthful, acknowledging the importance of other people in our lives. Young people desperately need to learn this lesson, but adults also find it hard to apologize to young people when we wrong them.

**Love rejoices in others' happiness.** Loving people do not mope around in jealousy or suspicion when others succeed. A mature person realizes that each human being is largely responsible for his or her own successes and failures. Consequently, there should be no room in the heart of a loving person for envy or ill will. In an affluent culture such as ours, young people need to learn this if they are to avoid becoming jealous and greedy.

**Love applies to oneself as much as to others.** Too many people confuse self-love with selfishness. Selfishness means getting one's way at the expense of one's personal growth or the growth of others; selfishness is therefore anti-love or, in the terms of religion, sinful. Self-love, on the other hand, means accepting oneself unconditionally, being committed to personal growth, forgiving oneself, and rejoicing in personal successes. When self-love is lacking, love for others is impossible; part of loving others requires that we believe we have something worth sharing with them. If our love for young people does not engender self-love in them, they will continue to travel the self-destructive road of dependency. We cannot make them love themselves, however; they must do this freely. The most we can do in this regard is help them make a connection between their lovableness and our love for them.

No adult can offer all of these qualities of love all the time, but most of us can offer a little bit some of the time. If we are not loving, then we'd best question just what it is we're doing with our lives. All the spiritual masters who have ever walked the earth, along with the best of scientists in the field of human behavior, acknowledge love to be the most essential of all human bahaviors. And when it comes to love and loving, a little bit often goes a long way. As Fr. John Powell aptly put it, "It only takes a moment to be loved a whole life through." How true! I am always amazed at how quickly even severely dehabilitated kids respond to love and how healthy they become when love is offered them consistently. If you wish to see miracles happen with young people, try loving in the manner just described.

**A Time for Decision**

Having reflected on the essential qualities of a habilitating adult role model—involvement and love—we must now ask ourselves if this is something we want to commit or re-commit ourselves to. We must then make a conscious decision to love and involve ourselves with young people. If you decide to do so, begin with the young people already rubbing shoulders with you. Perhaps later you will want to expand this circle.

Activity 1 was designed to help you determine where you are now in your involvements with young people. After identifying areas you'd like to improve, write yourself a letter of resolutions for the future, seal it in a self-addressed, stamped envelope, and ask a friend to drop it in the mail to you about a month from now. This will serve to remind you of your commitments to young people. If the resolution letter idea does not appeal to you, make a list of resolutions and tape it on your desk or another suitable place so you can refer to it from time to time. Your decision to be a loving, involved role model must be renewed frequently or your love will grow cold. Better yet, join or form a support group where adults come together to share their highs and lows in working with young people. Such a group offers an opportunity for support, exchange of views, and renewal of dedication.

**Questions for Reflection and Discussion**

1. What are some characteristics of a good adult role model?
2. Do you believe parents should be friends with their kids? Explain.

3. How do you feel about being a positive adult role model? Do you believe you're a good role model?
4. Give some examples of habilitative activities that can be enjoyed at home. At school.

## ACTIVITY 1
### Role-Modeling Evaluation

How frequently do you do the kinds of things described below?

Always (A); Usually (U); Seldom (S); Never (N).

| | A | U | S | N |
|---|---|---|---|---|
| 1. Do I project an image of being pleased to be involved with my young people? | | | | |
| 2. Do I address them using their preferred names? | | | | |
| 3. Do I discipline them by confronting their behaviors, but not putting their personalities down? | | | | |
| 4. Do I notice the good things they do and comment on them accordingly? | | | | |
| 5. Do I admit it when I make mistakes? | | | | |
| 6. Do I apologize to individuals when I wrong them? | | | | |
| 7. Do I express my feelings in appropriate ways when I am with young people? | | | | |
| 8. Do I encourage them in their interests? | | | | |

| | | A | U | S | N |
|---|---|---|---|---|---|
| 9. | Do I tell individuals I'm glad to see them when they've been away for awhile? | | | | |
| 10. | Do I find appropriate ways to affirm young people through physical touch? | | | | |
| 11. | Do I tell young people that I love them? | | | | |
| 12. | Do I discourage teasing among young people? | | | | |
| 13. | Do I help young people make decisions about sex, alcohol and drug use, and other health issues? | | | | |
| 14. | Do I avoid showing favoritism or attacking "victims"? | | | | |
| 15. | Am I clear about what is acceptable behavior? | | | | |
| 16. | Have I established logical and natural consequences for breaking group rules? | | | | |
| 17. | Do I help young people understand moral principles? | | | | |
| 18. | Do I help young people believe in the future? | | | | |
| 19. | Am I available to talk with young people about any problems they might need to discuss? | | | | |

| | A | U | S | N |
|---|---|---|---|---|
| 20. Am I willing to help young people discover God in their lives? | | | | |
| 21. Do I challenge unreasonable beliefs young people have about themselves? | | | | |
| 22. Do I encourage young people to make the most of their educational opportunities? | | | | |
| 23. Do I help young people learn to express their feelings in appropriate ways? | | | | |
| 24. Do I encourage young people to try new hobbies and experiences? | | | | |
| 25. Do I avoid comparing young people to one another? | | | | |

20 or more responses in Always/Usually range: positive role model. Thank you for being involved with young people!

12-19 responses in Always/Usually range: potentially good role model. With a little effort kids could really take a liking to you.

0-11 responses in Always/Usually range: poor role model. You have very little positive influence in the lives of young people.

3

# Communicating Self-Worth

Human beings are essentially relational in nature. What we come to believe about ourselves—our worth, our capabilities, and our limitations—is determined by an ongoing process of interaction in a world of people.

For the developing child, relationships with parents and other family members provide the most significant feedback in the formation of his or her self-concept. The child believes about him or herself what is said and implied by family members; they are mirrors reflecting back to the child a variety of messages about the child's worth. This feedback, along with the child's individual experiences of success and failure, helps to form emotional convictions about his or her self-concept in the unconscious depths of the psyche.

As a child grows older, feedback from teachers and from friends at school or in the neighborhood also help to influence self-concept development. Adolescents almost seem to value the opinions of peers more than they do the opinions of their parents, but the influence of home and family—for better or worse—is never completely lost. Gradually, through childhood and adolescence, each of us develops a core of beliefs about ourselves. This process continues all through life, but stabilizes considerably during our early twenties.

So far it might sound as though one's self-concept is determined totally by external factors (what others tell us about ourselves). This is not entirely true, however. Out of a wide variety of messages from others entering the mind as grist for self-concept development, only selected bits and pieces are retained as significant. Each of us decides which messages are to be considered seriously and which should be discarded; self-concept is as much what we choose to believe about ourselves as what others tell us. There is no doubt, however, that a child's self-concept is strongly biased in favor of feedback received from positive adult role models.

During adolescence and young adulthood, an intense search for the self ensues. Because of hormonal factors, our bodies begin to change and, with it, our understanding of our identity. We no longer look like children, so we begin to detach ourselves from our parents, who (for a short time, at least) continue in our perceptions to relate to us as though we were children. Because peers seem most likely to be sympathetic to our struggles, we turn to them with a vengeance, and they accept us because they're in the same boat.

Freed from the compulsion to seek gratification from parental approval, young people then begin to try on new identities by experimenting with different experiences. What these will be and how they will affect us depends in large part on the values about health we learned as small children. In fact, the very peer group chosen by a young person is a values-based decision; there are many kinds of peer groups to choose from, and young people will be drawn toward those groups most reflective of their own sense of values. What is important for adults to realize here is that this search for the self during adolescence is a normal part of growth; teenagers' confusion and restlessness is to be expected.

Self-concept, then, is determined by the quality of feedback we get from the significant people in our lives, by our individual experiences of success and failure, and by what we choose to believe about ourselves. The importance of this understanding cannot be overstated, for it points out areas in which we can work with young people to help them develop positive self-concepts. Young people who develop positive self-concepts are more likely to avoid destructive behavior and experience happiness than are those who dislike themselves. Keeping this in mind, we can go on to examine the role of positive adult role models in helping to habilitate young people all through their growing years.

When adults and young people spend time together engaged in significant activities at home or at school, the give and take of interaction communicates to each young person an evaluation of her or his personality and behavior. There is no such thing as a neutral relationship between young people and the parents, teachers, coaches, and other adults they spend lots of time with. Feedback from these significant adults will affect their self-concept for better or worse. So we see that those of us who work with kids have a tremendous responsibility to relate to them in a habilitative manner. We can communicate evaluations about self-concept to young people by three methods: affirmation, discipline, and shame.

## Affirmation

Affirmation is perhaps the greatest power on earth entrusted to human beings; unfortunately, it is treated with appalling neglect. By affirmation I mean communicating to another person a positive evaluation of his or her personality and behavior. Affirmation says "I like who you are and I like what you're doing." When internalized by the recipient, the message becomes "I am lovable and capable," which is a nice summary of the habilitated attitude. We are not talking about flattery here, for flattery is cheap and manipulative. Genuine affirmation must be sincere and from the heart; it is an expression of your appreciation for the good things that other people bring to your life.

Test yourself now to see how affirming you are on a day-to-day basis. Think of a young person (or an older one, as the case may be) with whom you are closely involved regularly. Write this person's name on a sheet of paper, then make a list titled "Things this person does that please me." Be specific as you go on to complete this list. Next, make another list, titled "Things this person does that displease me." When you are finished, look over both lists. Which one was harder to compile? Which behaviors have you commented on more over the past week or so? If you commented more on the pleasing behaviors, you are already on the road to becoming an affirming person.

Here are some examples of how to communicate affirmation.

*Your attitude* while interacting with young people is the most basic level of affirmation you can communicate. If you are glad to be where you are and to be interacting with the individuals around you, it will come across in various ways. If you do not feel this way most of the time, then you'd best work on your attitude. It makes a difference.

If you are like me, you were probably shocked to read in an Ann Landers survey that over 70 percent of parents with children said that they would go childless if they had to do it over again. How this attitude is affecting our children was brought home to me recently by a second-grade teacher I was working with. She had asked her students to share the question they would most like to ask their parents, and the results were sobering. "Are you glad you had me?" read one little boy's paper. "Was I a mistake?" read another's, already aware of the purpose of birth control and abortion. Here were children, the most glorious creations in God's universe, wondering if their parents really wanted them! One can only wonder about the parental attitudes in such homes. Attitudes about children make a difference.

*Using a young person's preferred name* is an affirming practice. Dale Carnegie wrote that no sound on earth is so special to a person as the sound of his own name. Call young people by name often when speaking to them. If nothing else, you will get better attention when you address them this way. You may even choose to allow them to call you by your own preferred name, minus the *Mr.* and *Mrs.* or whatever title you go by. Many adults believe this removes the condescension inherent in adult-youth relationships. Try it if you're comfortable with it and if it is permissible in your given setting. Because I work primarily in schools, where teachers are called *Mr.* or *Ms.* or *Mrs.*, I am usually unable to relate to students as just plain old Phil. But they do enjoy calling me "Mr. Phil" instead of "Mr. St. Romain"; I believe this slight informality helps to build relationships between us.

*Comment positively* on the things that young people do well. Young people cannot learn to believe in themselves and their abilities until other people—usually significant adults—believe in them first. Affirming the good they do as often as is appropriate (too much may seem cheap) helps to build in them confidence and an attitude of success.

Many of us were raised in households where affirmation was sparse. So long as we were doing what we were supposed to do, things were somewhat peaceful, but not necessarily appreciated. When we made mistakes or did something that was clearly wrong, we got plenty of attention from Mom and Dad, though. The rule in such households seems to be, "Do what you're supposed to do and all will be peaceful, but look out if you mess up!" Tragically, many teachers, parents, job supervisors, and others in positions of authority still operate from this position of negative correction/low affirmation. They have not yet realized that true power does not come from getting people to do what you want because they are afraid of you, but from motivating people to do something because they *want* to. If you want to help young people develop a healthy self-concept, affirm the good things they do, even if they've agreed to do them as necessary chores. Such affirmation works wonders with spouses and friends, too. How many of us take for granted the good things our loved ones do for us or for themselves daily? This is tragic! Resolve to find at least one thing to affirm in your loved ones today, and you will see the difference it makes.

*Help young people to learn to affirm themselves.* We must beware of making young people dependent on our affirmation. What is important is that they learn to value themselves and their talents for their own sake, not for yours. Help them to make the connection between their basic goodness and your praise.

For example, my daughter Theresa draws endless numbers of dolls, horses, and other assorted things. I have always tried to find very specific things to affirm in her pictures (purple hair, green mane) because with young children we must be very concrete about what we like, as opposed to saying just "That's nice" or "How beautiful." Then one day I realized that she had come to depend upon my approval of her pictures. My wife and I talked it over and decided to change tactics. Now, in addition to telling Theresa what we like about her pictures, we spend time asking her what *she* likes about them, trying to affirm her own perceptions. The ideal is that kids come to us saying not, "See what I've done; is it any good?" but "See the good thing I've done!"

*Expressing love* is another way to affirm people. What I have said so far about affirmation is part of loving people, but it is not all. The three simple words "I love you," spoken in sincerity by a significant adult, are life to young people.

Many would argue at this point that it is more important to act out of love than to tell others that they are loved. This is especially true if we offer words alone but fall short on loving deeds. But why not both, words *and* deeds?

In addition to telling young people occasionally that we love them, we can express our love for them through hugs, handshakes, and even kisses. Adolescents are especially loath to touch their parents and other adults, but they need physical assurances of affection just as much as the rest of us. I find most kids to be receptive to a pat on the back, an arm around the shoulders, and occasional touches on the arm. After a while, many even become accepting of a warm, welcoming hug. Such gestures communicate care in physical, concrete ways, which is the dimension of reality kids understand best.

Letting young people know through verbal or physical expressions that they are loved can and even should be done at the most insignificant times possible. Do not tell kids you love them only when they have experienced a success of some kind or have done something nice for you. If you do so, they will come to believe that they are loved for their behaviors, and they will fall into the nasty trap of trying to earn love. Love, if it is real, cannot be earned; it is a decision we make about other people and a gift we give to them. Young people who experience this kind of unconditional love from adults will probably never have to worry about their mental health.

The decision to become a more affirming person is one of the most important decisions you will ever make. The good news is that you will benefit from this practice as much as the young people you work with will. We become as we behave to some extent, and people who make a point of finding something good to say about others become warm, treasured friends. Furthermore, affirmation channels tremendous measures of spiritual power through us, bringing healing and confidence in our own minds. It sounds almost too good to be true, but a commitment to be an affirming person does require lots of hard work from us. Still, if you decide to make an effort to become an affirming person, you will never be short on friends or on happiness.

### Discipline

It is a myth that affirmation alone can nurture a young person to health and maturity. Young people are constantly testing adults' limits, pushing to see how much they can get away with. Their desire to please adults often seems (to them, at least) to be in conflict with their need for independence and spontaneity. This accounts for much of their rebellious acting out—deliberately avoiding their assigned chores, for example, or doing poorly in school even though they can do better. Often, too, peer influence leads them to say and do things they would never do alone. But regardless of the reasons why young people act irresponsibly at times, they must be confronted and disciplined when they do wrong, or else they will believe that you condone their misbehavior.

Because disciplining for responsibility requires considerable thought and discussion, this topic will be taken up in full in chapter 4. Suffice it to say for our purposes now that confrontation for the purpose of discipline is an evaluation of one's behavior, not personality. "I still like you, but right now I don't like what you're doing" is the message we should communicate when we discipline young people (or anyone, for that matter). Effective discipline presumes that we have been affirming, that we have rules concerning the behavior in question, and that consequences for misbehaving will be experienced. Making a plan to do better is another essential ingredient for habilitative disciplining.

Young people who are disciplined this way generally come to respect themselves and the adults working with them more deeply. They do not really respect adults who let them get away with irresponsible behavior, as is the case with many parents and teachers hung up on being "friends" with young people. Disciplining young people is part of calling them to growth, which is part of loving them.

## Shaming

The reason why disciplining kids has such a negative connotation in some circles is that we sometimes confuse it with shaming. Consequently, we often avoid necessary confrontations, thus "throwing out the baby with the bathwater." It is easy to avoid shaming, although the temptation to do so is sometimes hard to resist.

Shaming is a confrontation that addresses negative behavior, but also drags in negative comments on personality. In the recipient's perception, shaming comments are put-downs. Shaming says, "You're no good and you can't do anything right." When internalized, shaming comments are interpreted as "I am unlovable and incapable," the antithesis of the habilitated attitude. Young people who are shamed will not try to change destructive behaviors; they will become defensive and angry instead. Making shaming comments in front of a young person's friends will merit you his hatred and contempt. He will not be respectful of the rules and expectations you have for him. You *and* he will lose.

Most of us have been treated in shaming ways at some time; perhaps that is why we respond in kind when circumstances seem to justify this evaluation. When we shame others, we are usually reacting to external circumstances that infringe on our needs and wants. Tired parents and teachers who have to contend with cranky, unrelenting kids are especially likely to fall into this trap. But even in such times, maturity calls us to act, not react. If we simply react to circumstances, we are allowing control over our lives to be taken from us. We are then also likely to vent our frustrations in one of the shaming behaviors described here.

*Comparisons.* "You're just like your father." (This puts Dad down, too.) "Why can't you be more like your sister?" Comparisons imply that people are not acceptable as themselves.

*Labeling.* "She's a slow learner." "He's the black sheep of the family." Beware, too, of derogatory nicknames kids call one another. When such names are used, you must deal with it in a disciplinary manner. Even if the name seems funny, you can bet that the person being laughed at is feeling shamed.

*Dumping.* By this I mean unloading your anger and frustrations on young people when you are really mad about something else. Disproportionate anger is also a form of shaming.

*Condescension.* "Aren't you ever going to grow up?" No young person likes this question. Of course, no adult likes to be treated with condescension, either. In a recent armchair philosophy discussion about world affairs, a man who disagreed with what I was saying blew up and proceeded to lecture at me. When his wife called him down about it, he replied, "Someone's got to teach this little know-it-all about how the world really works!" Even though I have a pretty healthy self-concept, the shaming comments of this man almost moved me to act in a vindictive, undignified manner. When we treat young people as though they have no sense, they feel the same way.

*Judgmentalism.* There is a vast difference between a disciplinary confrontation and a judgmental put-down. Judgments are statements about people's motives, and no one ever really knows another's motives. That is why Jesus told us not to judge; in fact, when we judge others, we are revealing something about our own motives—hence, we really judge ourselves. Common judgmental statements are "You only care about yourself" and "You just don't want to learn, do you?" Using generalizations ("You always...," "You never...") also smacks of judgmentalism.

*Profanity.* "When you get angry, count to four; when you get very angry, swear." This quip from Mark Twain is humorous, but swearing at young people is not. Because profanity is often used by the inarticulate of this world to express especially negative sentiments, swearing at young people is usually perceived as a put-down.

*Negative attitudes.* This is the most basic level of shaming, communicating to kids a message that says "I'm not glad to be here and I'm not glad you're here either." They pick up on this one quickly. Teachers who constantly complain about their jobs in front of their students and parents who spend lots of time being angry with their kids send out this message.

*Neglect.* We demonstrate neglect when we do not spend time with young people, or listen to them, or discipline them. Adults who neglect young people are really saying "You're so unimportant, I won't even pay attention to you." The opposite of love is not hate, but apathy, and neglect is a form of apathy. This form of shaming is perhaps the most common of all.

I know a high school sophomore, Jeff, who lives at home alone with his mother. Jeff's mother works nights and sleeps during the day when Jeff is at school. After Jeff received his driver's license, he began to get into trouble because of drinking, speeding, and riding around with a group of troublemakers. This unsupervised lifestyle began to affect his schoolwork, but we never could get Jeff's mother to come in and talk about it. Surely her lack of involvement in her son's life is part of his problem.

We have children who begin school with a vocabulary of less than 400 words because no one has spent much time talking with them. Other children eat their only well-balanced meals at school. The most common form of neglect, however, is the type experienced by Jeff. Maybe educators alone are aware of the thousands of young people who have little or no adult supervision after school hours. Sometimes this situation is a consequence of their parents' work schedule. But far too often, there is no reason for it except lack of care.

You get the idea. As you may have noticed, shaming remarks have absolutely nothing in their favor. Whatever motivation to change we might be able to encourage with this kind of evaluation is offset by damage to the ego. Shaming is always counterproductive.

Most of us make shaming evaluations out of our own frustrations and low self-worth. Seldom do we actually intend the kind of put-down that shaming behavior communicates. We're usually just reacting to a disturbance and trying to buy a little peace and quiet for ourselves. But shaming must be completely eliminated from the lives of all who are trying to habilitate young people. We must make a conscious commitment today to begin identifying any shaming practices that we use consciously or unconsciously against young people.

There is no excuse for shaming kids; disciplinary confrontations are far more effective in helping them change destructive behaviors, and there are far healthier ways for us to express our own feelings. In fact, if a person finds that, for whatever reasons, he or she cannot avoid shaming young people, it would be better not to work with them at all.

## Special Problems

Many dependent young people have a shame-based self-concept. They do not believe in their worth as human beings, and they are not responsible or disciplined. They act out their feelings and do destructive things to gain negative attention—which, after all, is better than no attention at all. Leading these kids toward habilitation requires a tremendous amount of patience and persistence in affirmation. Sometimes they do not even seem to accept affirmation at first, and they may perceive your disciplinary efforts as shaming. They have been shamed for so long that when you confront them with "You've done something wrong," their mental tape recorder automatically spins out the corollary, "Therefore I'm no good." It is not your fault that such kids shame themselves. Persist as best you can in affirming and disciplining them, but do not hesitate to seek professional help for those who seem unable to get out of their self-hating behaviors. No one adult can ever provide complete care for a young person. It takes a network of caring adults to habilitate youth, and you are certainly no failure for admitting that you need help from time to time.

### Questions for Reflection and Discussion

1. Why is it important to affirm people?
2. What are some of the ways that you affirm the young people you work with?
3. Why is shaming so counterproductive?
4. What is the difference between shaming and disciplining?
5. What are some of the ways in which young people are shamed today?

4

# Disciplining for Responsibility

"Spare the rod and spoil the child" reads a Biblical proverb often invoked by people to justify their harsh treatment of young people. I have heard many school principals and teachers lament their loss of spanking privileges as though this were the best way to discipline kids. In fact, most adults subscribe to a notion of discipline that is really more like punishment.

There is a difference between punishment and discipline. Punishment means influencing behavior by using the threat of pain. "Do this or else . . ." is the sentiment conveyed. It might be appropriate to use punishment in institutions like prisons where people are sent to atone for misdeeds, but certainly not in our schools and homes. Discipline, on the other hand, means influencing behavior according to reasonable rules that make life better for all concerned. "Do this so that we can better enjoy . . . " is the stance of discipline. Those who break these rules may have to experience the consequences, but even here discipline emphasizes a return to the community and to reasonableness rather than the threat of pain.

People who believe that punishment is the best way to teach responsibility have a very cynical view of human nature. I recall a recent meeting of parents when an older man stood up and objected to my criticism of punishment, saying, "I whip my kids and they'd better turn out OK." My response to him was, "Who will whip them when they leave home?" And that, it seems to me, summarizes the difference between discipline and punishment.

Punishment requires the presence of an external authority to impose sanctions on rule offenders; it is external-oriented. Discipline teaches decision-making for one's own good. People who are punished grow up thinking that what makes something acceptable or non-acceptable is the likelihood of getting caught at it. According to Dr. Lawrence Kohlberg, whose work in moral development is internationally acclaimed, the fear of punishment represents a very primitive level of morality. Societies based on a fear-of-punishment ethic are unstable police states; societies based on discipline respect freedom, but recognize the value of rules that help us to live together in peace.

Punishing young people is really just another form of shaming them. Punishing people is an attempt to condition their behavior as we would an animal's. If we want to teach responsibility, then we need to recognize that disciplining young people is infinitely preferable to behavior modification through punishment.

The guidelines for discipline discussed below have been taught by a variety of experts in education, parenting, and spiritual growth for decades. In truth, they are little more than common sense, but they still must be studied and implemented if they are to work for us.

### Create a Vital Community

If our homes, schools, churches, teams, bands, and other groups are places where young people more or less want to be, it will be easy to discipline them. Creating such a community is the primary challenge of adults who live and work with young people. If kids do not want to be part of these groups, we will have to resort to punishment to keep them in. Young people who run away from home or drop out of school obviously do not value these communities. When we listen to some of their stories, it is easy to understand why.

Billy, age 11, was transferred to a school I work with in the middle of the fall semester. He was thin and appeared to be nervous, but he got along fairly well for awhile until one day he refused to dress out for P.E. When his teacher pressed him to do so, Billy began crying. The teacher took him aside to talk about it, and Billy protested that he couldn't play football that day because his legs were hurting. This was a sure tip-off that something was wrong with Billy that he did not want to discuss. The teacher took him to the rest room to observe the source of Billy's pain and there discovered several fresh belt bruises on his legs and thighs. We learned later that day that Billy's father beat him, his mother, and his younger sister regularly. In addition, Billy suspected that his father was having sex with his 16-year-old sister. She would confess to none of it, but later the child protection authorities had all three children moved out of this home.

Many young people grow up in turbulent homes like Billy's. We have over 10 million untreated chemically dependent people in our country, and life can be very crazy in these families. Young people never know what mood their parents will be in. "Will they be angry, will they fight, will they blame me for something?" they often wonder. But the home community isn't the only place they feel oppressed. I know of teachers who were caught molesting their students, and even one sad case where a minister was molesting the young boys who worked with him in church. Adults who do these kinds of things create an environment where effective discipline is simply not possible.

We create a vital community by practicing the loving behavior discussed in this book. Young people will feel a sense of belonging in any group where they are listened to, taken seriously, encouraged to dream, affirmed in the good they do, cautioned against destructive influences, and involved in meaningful activities. Creative adults will recognize here the almost infinite number of ways in which these values can become part of group life. This sense of belonging is our lever for disciplining young people, without which the remaining steps cannot work effectively.

### Establish Reasonable Rules

Order is generally preferable to disorder, and a few reasonable rules can help any group maximize its strengths and minimize its weaknesses. Note the use of the word *reasonable*, however. Rules imposed arbitrarily and for no apparent purpose are likely to be ignored and disobeyed. Such rules are largely responsible for the ennui and apathy prevailing in many private and public institutions today. Arbitrary, unreasonable rules do nothing to improve the quality of life shared by people in the home, classroom, and on the job.

*Non-negotiable reasonable rules* are rules that are unilaterally imposed by authorities. Parents and teachers, for example, have a right to demand from young people certain behaviors for the good of the family and classroom, respectively. Non-negotiable rules in the home might include school attendance, daily bath or shower, weekly church attendance, courteous speech, and abstinence from alcohol and drugs. These are laid down for the good of the young people in the family by parents who are morally and legally responsible for the growth and development of their children. Schools usually insist on punctuality, bringing necessary materials to class, staying on campus during school hours, nonviolent behavior, and abstinence from alcohol and drugs on campus. Even though such rules are non-negotiable, they are still reasonable.

*Negotiable rules* are worked out through dialogue between adults and young people. The timing of chores, study hours, and recreation usually requires a certain amount of flexibility. Teachers, too, can find numerous instances when students can be included in making rules and decisions about classroom life. In fact, the ideal would be for all rules to be negotiables worked out in dialogue, for young people are more likely to follow rules they formulate than those imposed on them by authorities.

If young people participate with you in a vital community, it should be easier for them to reach agreement on the value of reasonable rules. Discuss your group's rules occasionally. Ask for a show of hands from all who agree with the rules in question. Let them write about or discuss the reasons why these rules exist. Ask them to complete open-ended statements like "If we didn't have this rule, then our group might . . . " If they perceive disciplinary rules as reasonable, they are more likely to be committed to them.

### Agree on Consequences for Breaking Rules

Even after affirming young people and doing everything possible to build a vital community supported by reasonable rules, you can be certain that some individuals will break the rules occasionally. Young people break rules out of ignorance, forgetfulness, poor judgment, and sometimes even rebelliousness. Regardless of the reasons why a rule is broken—and kids will usually give you some very good reasons for breaking rules—it is your duty to see that rule-breakers experience some kind of consequences for their behavior. It is important, too, that these consequences not be considered punishments, but measures to help teach lessons and strengthen individual and group discipline. There are three types of consequences people may experience after breaking a rule.

*Arbitrary consequences* are punitive in nature, generally having no connection at all to the rule in question. Spankings and other forms of physical and verbal abuse are examples of arbitrary consequences. They teach no lesson except the lesson that the one who renders the abuse ought to be feared—and then only at certain times, such as when he or she is in a bad mood. Arbitrary consequences are usually examples of shaming, for they do not recognize the fact that people have minds that can usually find other ways of behaving without the threat of pain hovering over them.

*Natural consequences,* on the other hand—simply allowing things to run their course—can be the best disciplinary teachers. For example, a child who forgets to bring his lunch to school should be allowed to borrow from friends or else miss a meal; he will not die from this, and he might learn a lesson from it. Similarly, those who forget to dress warmly in cold weather ought to be allowed to experience getting cold (except for small children in very cold weather, of course). Capable grownups who do not work suffer deprivations in food, clothing, shelter, and health care, but most caring adults find it extremely difficult to watch young people learn lessons from natural consequences. Our general tendency is to rescue them by giving reminders or directions or by checking up on them, usually in the name of love. This is understandable, but we must realize that allowing young people to experience a few lumps and bruises in life may be the more loving way.

However, it is sometimes too risky to allow young people to learn lessons from natural consequences. No one wants to let toddlers learn the dangers of crossing busy streets by experiencing natural consequences. Also, we must make rules regarding alcohol and drug use, because the consequences of abuse in this area could cost lives and good health. Natural consequences work best when appropriate, but they are not always the prudent way to teach lessons.

*Logical consequences* are artificial in the sense that nature does not impose them, but they are helpful because they teach lessons without being punitive. Ideally, a logical consequence is directly related to a reasonable rule. A few examples: refusing classroom admittance to a student who has, without a good excuse, broken your rule about being in class on time; withholding new toys from a toddler until he puts away the toys he's just finished playing with; grounding a teenager for two weeks after she has broken your house rule about curfews; keeping students who misbehave during classtime in for recess so that they can catch up on work they missed while fooling around in class; and revoking a teenager's car use privileges for two months after he gets a speeding ticket. Activities 2, 3, and 4 at the end of this chapter suggest ways to set up a system of logical consequences in the home and at school.

If these kinds of consequences can be agreed upon when

the rules are spelled out, then your role is to honor the choices your young people have made. The choices are theirs: either obey the rules or suffer the loss of certain contingent privileges until they earn their way back to privileged status.

The manner in which logical consequences can be used in disciplining is illustrated in the following example. Let us suppose that a mother and her 15-year-old daughter have reached agreement on a few rules concerning the daughter's going out at night with her friends. She is to abstain from alcohol and drugs, be home by 11 P.M., and inform her parents where she will be going and with whom. If she breaks any of these rules, she will be grounded for two weeks and will be assigned extra chores at home. Friday night comes, and the daughter returns home at 11:30 P.M. with alcohol on her breath. Let's listen in.

*Mother:* You're home. Thank goodness you're safe! I was worried about you.

*Daughter:* I was only at Judy's like I told you! Jerry wouldn't leave on time. I'm sorry I'm late. Will you forgive me?

*Mother:* Of course I forgive you, but you could have called.

*Daughter:* Their phone was out. Besides, I'm not that late.

*Mother:* You've been drinking, too, haven't you?

*Daughter* (exasperated): Mom! I only had a sip of Jerry's wine. It's no big deal!

*Mother:* Do you think it will be a big deal when you miss Lucy's party tomorrow night?

*Daughter:* What do you mean?

*Mother:* We had an agreement and you broke it by drinking, coming in late, and not calling. I now have to respect your decision to stay home for two weeks and take on more chores. Maybe we can even repaint that old desk you want to bring up in your room.

*Daughter:* It's not fair, Mom! They're expecting me at Lucy's tomorrow night. I can't just miss it. I thought you said you forgave me.

*Mother:* You let your friends down tonight, not me. And I do forgive you; I won't even mention it again. But I think it's important now for me to respect the agreements we made about your going out. Wouldn't it be terrible if I did not keep my half of our agreements?

What is important to note in the above dialogue is the respect that the mother shows for her daughter's decision. The daughter brought the problem upon herself, and it is likely that she learned a lesson from it. Furthermore, the mother avoided falling into the role of the "heavy." She was simply honoring an agreement made in good faith with her daughter, which left them both feeling more dignified than if an exchange of blaming and shaming remarks had ensued.

A few words about spanking seem in order now, especially since we opened this chapter with the Biblical proverb about the rod. Spanking is clearly a punitive measure, but it may be appropriate at times for very young children who do not yet appreciate the value of community or understand the importance of reasonable rules. You may tell an 18-month-old child that going out into the street is dangerous, and you may promise logical consequences if your non-negotiable rule is broken, but it is doubtful that a child this young will remember these things for long. Even so, spankings should never be administered out of your own anger and should always be the result of the breaking of a reasonable rule. It is my belief, too, that children over three years of age are capable of understanding simple rules, so spanking them ought to be unnecessary. Whipping teenagers is especially uncalled for, although many parents and teachers believe it's the only thing they understand. Remember, the Biblical proverb refers to a child, and adolescents are not children—although they are not adults, either.

### Enforce Consequences When Rules Are Broken

This step is self-explanatory. Be sure to avoid falling into the role of the "heavy," however. When you enforce consequences, let it be known that you are simply honoring the choices made by your young people.

### Make a Plan to Do Better

Healthy young people occasionally break reasonable rules, but natural and logical consequences usually help to get them back in line quickly. Kids who break rules frequently may have problems that require more than just the imposition of consequences to straighten out. Shame-based kids, for example, are not as likely to feel a part of your community and so will not appreciate the value of reasonable rules. They are likely to perceive consequences as punishment, thus deepening their sense of worthlessness. In such cases, making a plan to do better might include regular visits with a counselor.

Frequent rule-breaking can sometimes be diminished by changing a few external circumstances. Teachers discovered long ago the value of breaking up groups of talkers or moving a misbehaving student to a front seat. Parents are asking for trouble when they leave breakable items within the reach of toddlers. Perhaps the liquor cabinet ought to be locked when teenagers have friends over. A student who constantly forgets to bring a pencil to school might leave one in the classroom. Children who keep their rooms messy might benefit from your going through their things with them and throwing away unnecessary items while designating storage places for items they want to keep.

If you find that a majority of young people break your rules regularly, it may be that the rules are unreasonable or the kids do not yet possess the necessary cognitive skills to keep them faithfully. I remember the case of two students who were continually receiving tardy slips for their third-hour class on Tuesdays—so much so that they were suspended for it once. When their teacher finally checked into it, he discovered that their P.E. coach had them picking up the volleyball equipment on Tuesdays; they simply did not have enough time to do this, change clothes, and cross campus in time for their next class. The coach was notified of the problem, and thereafter he allowed the students to change clothes earlier than the rest of the class.

## Be Consistent

Never let favoritism or your moods determine how you impose consequences. We are only human, of course, and absolute consistency is an unattainable goal. But it is an important ideal to strive for; without consistency, discipline will break down to some extent.

Discipline is the duty of every adult who works with young people. In every human community that young people will ever belong to, whether it be for work or play, there are rules, and these rules usually help to strengthen the community. If we succeed in impressing upon young people the importance of discipline, they will eventually become self-disciplined—capable of recognizing for themselves the rules for behavior that strengthen them and the communities of which they are a part. If an overwhelming majority of today's young people were to learn these lessons, we would find oursleves on the threshold of a just and peaceful society.

## Questions for Reflection and Discussion

1. What is the difference between punishment and discipline?
2. Why is it so important to have a strong community if discipline is to work?
3. How do you feel about spanking young children?
4. How are you at using natural and logical consequences in your everyday disciplining?
5. What kinds of rules do you negotiate with young people?

## ACTIVITY 2

### The Family Time-Out Space

**Problem.** How to discipline children two years and older who persist in whining or acting cranky when they cannot get their way.

**Values at stake.** Crying is an appropriate way to express sadness, pain, and fear; it is inappropriate to cry for not getting one's way. Furthermore, such whining disturbs other people, who have a right to a peaceful environment. Verbal communication is the more effective way for people to negotiate their needs and wants.

**Strategies:**

1. Designate a room, chair, or any place in your home as a time-out space. It is preferable for this place to be in open view of normal family activities. Do not use the child's room, for you want that space to be associated with rest and play.

2. Do not let the child succeed in manipulating you through whining. It is important that you make it clear that this will not bring him what he wants.

3. Make a sincere attempt to communicate with the child. Are the child's needs or wants legitimate? Are your expectations reasonable?

4. If the child is persistently obstinate, bring the child to the time-out space and tell him that he must remain there until the crying ceases and the child is ready to communicate or fulfull the necessary responsibilities.

5. Allow the child to cry, scream, and vent feelings, but pay no attention to this unless physical or verbal abuse ensues.

6. After a few minutes, take the initiative of inviting the child to do what is necessary to resume normal activities. Let him know you still love him.

7. If the child leaves the space before meeting your conditions, simply bring him back and explain the situation again.

## ACTIVITY 3

### Handling Teenagers' Accountability and Social Activities

**Problem.** How to help ensure the safety of your teenagers when they go out with friends.

**Values at stake.** It is important that teenagers experience opportunities to socialize informally with their friends. As a parent or guardian, however, you are morally and legally responsible for their welfare. But you need their cooperation if they are to have social activities safely.

**Strategies:**

1. Let it be known that you want to see your teenagers have a variety of social experiences, but that you are also deeply concerned about their health.
2. Establish negotiable and non-negotiable rules concerning going out. These rules should address curfew limits, chaperones, alcohol/drug usage, and fulfillment of responsibilities at home before they can leave.
3. Invite your teenagers to agree to the reasonableness of these rules for your sake and theirs.
4. Let your teenagers know that infringements of these rules on purpose and without prior discussion will result in the loss of the opportunity to go out again for a certain period of time. Furthermore, this grounding will be supplemented by increased responsibilities at home to strengthen them for their next brush with temptation.
5. Act surprised when they break the agreed-upon rules. Let them know you will now have to honor their decision to stay home and work harder for a few days until they earn back the opportunity to go out.

## ACTIVITY 4
### Improving Classroom Discipline

**Problem.** How to allow students to experience consequences for a wide variety of disciplinary problems.

**Values at stake.** Students exhibit a wide range of undisciplined behavior in the classroom and on the school grounds. They need to know which specific behaviors are considered unacceptable and what the consequences will be for misbehaving. They also need to learn that certain behaviors are more disruptive than others, and that the consequences for serious disruptions will be more serious than for minor disturbances.

***Strategies:***

1. Let students know that it is your desire to teach as interesting and stimulating a class as possible, but that to do so will require cooperation from them.

2. Share with students the school's rules (nonnegotiables); negotiate additional rules to help meet your needs and theirs.

3. Establish consequences on the basis of demerit points:

10 points—minor disturbances (forgetting books, leaving seat without permission, talking out of turn, chewing gum, cutting up in lunch line, etc.)

25 points—major disturbances (arguing with teacher, unexcused tardiness, distracting class with humor, loud interruptions, teasing another student, etc.)

40 points—serious infractions (leaving campus without permission, scuffles on playground, minor thefts, etc.)

75 points—suspendable behaviors (possession or use of alcohol, tobacco, or other drugs, carrying a concealed weapon, fighting, etc.)

4. Enforce consequences:

25 points or more—recess or after-school detention with

work designed to help improve discipline in the area of concern.

40 points or more—note home to parents describing specific problems and requesting help and support; conference between student and principal or guidance counselor.

75 points or more—suspension for specified period of time. Many school policies call for expulsion for criminal acts.

5. Promise to reward students who remain under 25 demerit points. Be creative in deciding what this might be.

6. Be sure to tell students exactly where they stand upon request.

7. Reset demerit points after each six-or nine-week grading period.

# 5

# Reaching for the Stars

My work as a substance abuse prevention consultant for the Louisiana Department of Education involved considerable contact with teachers who have been trained to work in their schools on substance abuse prevention teams. These teachers have taught me much about young people today. Some of the older teachers have been especially helpful, because their experiences enable me to see today's young people in a wider perspective. One of these teachers, whom I shall call Mrs. Peterson, has always enjoyed good rapport with her home economics students. We can learn much from her.

Mrs. Peterson has been teaching for almost 30 years and is considered by her colleagues—many of whom she had taught—to be one of the best in the field. When she said, "Kids today just aren't motivated to learn like they used to be," I knew she was speaking from a wealth of experience. She went on to tell me that "the best teaching materials in the newest schools with the best-trained teachers" couldn't interest most kids in getting an education. Countless surveys of teachers confirm her point; motivating students to learn is the area where technical assistance is most often requested. As Mrs. Peterson put it, "If they wanted to learn, there are still plenty of things we could teach them."

**Why Don't They Care?**

There can be no doubt that part of teaching consists of motivating kids to learn. A good teacher is one who manages to arouse interest in the material being taught. But too many good teachers like Mrs. Peterson are experiencing great frustration with today's students. One of the biggest problems in education today is the mass exodus of good teachers from the classroom, many times in favor of lower-paying jobs. Teacher frustration seems to be at an all-time high, mostly because of the perception among teachers that working with today's kids is an unrewarding task. When, day after day, teachers find young people unwilling to learn and disinterested in school, they begin to feel as though they're just wasting their time.

The problem of unmotivated kids is very complex. The following factors have been implicated in several studies.

*They watched too much television as preschoolers* and therefore did not develop the imaginative skills necessary to enjoy reading. Reading is the key to education, and it is the skill in which many students today seem to be most deficient. In addition, many of the young people who do know how to read do not like to read because it is not interesting to them. They would rather watch television to get a story than plow through a book. Reading requires a lively imagination; it is an active, not a passive, involvement. The 1980 government report *Television and Behavior* pointed out quite clearly that television lowers the imaginative skills of preschoolers. It follows that young people with less-developed imaginations will enjoy reading less and hence will be less motivated to perform in an educational environment that depends heavily on reading.

*Many high schoolers use alcohol and other drugs,*

which diminishes motivation. We used to think that it was the other way around—that young people abused chemical substances because they were poorly motivated and somewhat bored with life. This may be true in some cases, but there is no longer any doubt that regular use of alcohol and, especially, marijuana diminishes a young person's interest in natural highs. Learning is a natural high, but one that requires considerable discipline and effort to experience. Why bother to learn or do anything active to make yourself happy when a drink or toke will give you similar feelings for no effort? It's like getting paid for doing nothing. But the will eventually goes lax through disuse; as the saying goes, "If you don't use it, you lose it." That's why most young people who get high regularly do poorly in school.

*Large classes* make it difficult for teachers to provide the personal attention necessary to help motivate young people to learn. It is rare to find a secondary school class with less than 25 students. Tight budgets have accounted for part of this predicament; it's cheaper to hire fewer teachers and increase class sizes than to provide additional classrooms and personnel to work with smaller groups. I was fortunate enough to receive my high school education in a small town. My graduating class numbered 24. Many of my elective courses included only about 15 students, and the rapport we had with our teachers was fantastic. They knew who we were, cared about us, and could provide the attention we needed when necessary. But what a shock it was when I went to college and walked into my freshman biology class! There were over 200 students sitting in an immense classroom. Needless to say, the professor never learned our names. But most college students are at least capable of motivating themselves to learn and have learned the basics of reading and writing, although more and more universities are providing remedial classes in even these key areas. Primary and secondary students are a different matter, however; they need involvement with their teachers if they are to learn.

*Parents do not require their young people to do homework like they used to.* My wife, an elementary school teacher, is constantly surprised at how many parents call her to complain about the amount of homework she sends home with her students. Remember when parents felt cheated when their kids came home with no homework? Of course, for many young people the situation with their parents has deteriorated to such an extent that they have little involvement of any kind with them, and certainly not enough for Mom or Dad to get on them about homework. When young people come home to an empty house and then are permitted to run around with little accountability, homework will surely be neglected. This is the case in more families now than at any time in our history. If teachers receive no support from parents regarding homework, discipline, and other educational issues, we can expect schools to be less successful than they could be. And that is precisely the case today.

*Young people have poorly focused personal dreams for their future;* therefore, for most of them, school seems to be irrelevant. This was not the case back in the '30s and '40s, when education was viewed as the best way to a higher-quality lifestyle. Young men who put in hours of hard physical labor each day hauling hay and slopping pigs did not have to be forced into school; the alternatives to bettering their lives through education were quite clear to them. Similarly, young women learned that the only way to a gratifying career is education. But what about today, when most young people don't have a lick of work to do at home? In our welfare state, young people know that those who don't work will nonetheless be given the basics for survival. It is therefore harder than ever to challenge young people to work hard in school; only those who have developed a personal dream that requires education to reach are easy to motivate. The rest do not realize the practical value of education, much less its broadening influences.

During the course of this book, we will touch on these issues in more detail. In this chapter, we need to examine the role of one's personal dreams for the future; this single factor seems most important in motivating young people to grow.

**Identifying the Ego-Ideal**

To understand what is meant by personal growth, it is necessary to discuss a few basic terms.

The *ego* is the conscious self in the present moment of existance. "I am . . . " is the ego's attitudinal state. It is the decision-making center of the psyche and is ultimately responsible for the direction we choose to go in life. The strong ego that comes from affirmation (chapter 3) helps young people make quality decisions about their lives.

The *superego* is the aspect of the psyche that includes directives from parents, teachers, and other authorities. "I should . . . " is its attitude. An unhealthy superego may seem more like an oppressive censor than a valuable guide. We instill a healthy superego in young people by disciplining them (chapter 4).

The *ego-ideal* is the self we would like to become. This dream person may be based on adult role models, but may also represent a unique personal dream. "I want to become . . . " is its attitude. A description of how to form a sound ego-ideal follows in the next section.

There are other important aspects of the psyche, of

course, but we shall limit our discussion to the above three. We can describe the ego as the conscious self, the superego as the should self, and the ego-ideal as the dream self. I define personal growth as directing your conscious self toward becoming your dream self.

**Formation of the Ego-Ideal**

The dream self or ego-ideal is an aspect of the psyche that is very active in children, but sadly idle in adults. Small children often pretend to be baseball players, ballet dancers, astronauts, or whatever they would like to become. Adolescence is also a time characterized by strong dreams and hopes for the future (in healthy young people, that is). During our twenties, we finally have the opportunity not only to prepare ourselves for living out our dreams, but also to actually begin experiencing those dreams. Unfortunately, this is also the time of life when the dream self begins to die. A characteristic statement describing this psychological death is, "I used to be an idealist, but now I am a realist." The movie *The Big Chill* brings this situation home forcefully. After about fifteen years of separation, the characters meet to mourn the suicide of one of their old 1960s gang. They remain together for the weekend and discover that they have all lost the idealism that had brought them together. "What has happened to us?" they lament. The answer: they have traded their idealism for the world's standards of materialistic success. The suicide provides a forceful and symbolic statement of the emptiness and unhappiness that they all feel.

The conscious self is directed primarily by either the should self or the dream self. By and large, we make decisions in response to *shoulds* and *oughts* or in pursuit of dreams and ideals. If the dream self dies, a person usually falls prey to the superego and begins living a life of *shoulds* or allows the ego to fade into the unconscious. Instinct and emotion then begin to dominate; the conscious self no longer makes decisions on the basis of values and reason. In such a condition, one no longer acts upon circumstances, but reacts to them. The difference between people who are growing and people who are regressing into the superego and into unconscious attitudes is striking. Regressives are generally dull, humorless, and somewhat cynical; growing people whose ego-ideals are still lively are warm, self-accepting, and fun-loving. Thus the cultivation of a healthy ego-ideal is an essential part of a full and fulfilling life.

But how do we "get" an ego-ideal? How can we help young people discover their own ego-ideals? Most importantly, how do we keep a dream self from being overwhelmed by the dreams imposed by a materialistic, hedonistic culture?

First of all, let us acknowledge the two primary sources of the ego-ideal: heroes and personal dreams. Heroes are important food for the formation of the ideal self. Small children often dream of becoming like their parents. During adolescence, they may idolize a coach, an aunt, or a rock star, often changing heroes as they try out different identities. By young adulthood, however, heroes are few, sometimes even non-existent. Young adults have discovered that all heroes are fallible and human, and their conversion from idealism to realism follows. It is during young adulthood that the role of religious heroes or abstract values can emerge as the new inspiration for the ideal self. Young adults who do not merge their own personal dreams with such universal heroes and principles seem destined to experience the death of the ego-ideal. When this happens, the superego embraces the world's standards of success and begins the pursuit of material wealth, comfort, and sensual pleasures.

Personal dreams arising from our own individuality are often quite different from the dreams inspired by our heroes. Sometimes, however, a hero sparks a personal dream that eclipses the original dream and launches us on a different journey. Personal dreams seem to be a spontaneous production of the psyche, manifesting themselves in nightly dreams, daydreams, and directed imagination. They reveal to us the purpose of our own individual destinies, and so ought to be treasured.

In an exciting book called *Dreams and Spiritual Growth,* authors Louis Savary, Patricia H. Bernes, and Stephen Kaplan Williams discuss destiny dreams and their importance for young people. They recount an instance of a man who, as a child, often dreamed of looking down into a grave with concern rather than dread. In his present profession, the man works with terminally ill people. His childhood dreams shaped the road he would take later on. I myself often dreamed of being a teacher when I was young; however, at that time in my life I thought I'd had enough of the school environment. But years later, after I'd tried my hand at a few other professions, I realized that I am indeed happy when helping other people learn, and my life began to fall into place. These kinds of personal dreams are precious, but they are also very fragile. They can be censored by the superego and ignored by the conscious self. If neglectd for too long, they may even die, or emerge only as fragments lacking any significant emotional charge.

### Helping Kids to Dream

This chapter has been more theoretical than the others because I believe that we must understand the importance of the dream self in personal growth. Without a vital dream self, people may feel lovable and capable, but they will not necessarily feel motivated to do anything with their lives. Needless to say, most dependent young people have had their dream selves crushed early in life because of shaming. It is nearly impossible to motivate these kids to "make something of themselves." Time, affirmation, discipline, and healthy involvements can help dependent young people develop a base from which new dreams may grow.

The role of the dream self can also be appreciated by observing those inspiring individuals who had everything going against them, but who rose to the top anyway because they dared to follow their dreams. Abraham Lincoln became president of the United States even though he was born into abject poverty. The Reverend Jesse Jackson, a leading spokesman for blacks today, was an illegitimate child who grew up in a poor, unstable family situation. And let us not forget Helen Keller, a beloved poet and philosopher, who was blind, deaf, and mute. Jackie Robinson, considered the first black to play major league baseball, succeeded immensely despite tremendous pressure and criticism. Finally, Christianity presents us with Jesus of Nazareth, a poor Jewish carpenter's son whose birth we use to mark history. These were people who dared to dream; their successes teach us that fidelity to our own dreams can lead us to growth and happiness.

Significant adults can do several important things to help young people embrace and cultivate their dream selves.

*Help young people believe in the future.* Without a future to hope for, dreams die, and many young people do not believe there is a future for them. They believe the world will blow up in a nuclear war, or that pollution and overpopulation will snuff out their plans. Everywhere they turn, the media and others are pointing out the dangers of nuclear holocaust. Even a small exchange between the superpowers, experts say, would send up enough dust to cool the earth and bring on a "nuclear winter." This may well happen, but it also may not. We have somehow managed to avoid nuclear holocaust over the past four decades; perhaps we shall continue to do so until the day when governments do away with nuclear bombs or develop new defense systems that render bombs obsolete. In the meantime, life must go on, and we must continue to hope that there will be a future for our children. The biggest mistake of all would be to abandon hope, for we would then be left with only the present and the past; we would begin to live only for today or only in the past.

One of the most powerful examples of hoping and striving I can recall was in the movie *The Other Side of the Mountain*. One of the young men in the hospital ward depicted in the film had a terminal illness, but he was working hard on his master's degree. When asked why he was going through all that trouble since he would be dead within a couple of years, he replied that he was doing it for himself and not for the practical use he might make of it. That's the kind of spirit we need to instill in our young people today.

*Talk to kids about their heroes.* Simple questions like "My favorite person is . . . " or "The person I would like most to be like is . . . " will yield incredibly fruitful conversations with young people. Ask them, too, why they chose their heroes. Tell them about the people who were your heroes when you were young.

*Encourage young poeple to share their personal dreams with you.* What are their interests, hobbies, and practical talents? Let them tell you their perceptions of these skills and interests, then affirm their perceptions and add your own. Invite them to tell you of their hopes for the future. Ask adolescents to write out for you their ideal job description.

*Use values clarification exercises with young people.* Many excellent books include formal activities for the home and classroom, but you can surely invent your own as you need to. My two daughters and I enjoy playing a simple game we call "Which Do You Prefer?" I give them a choice between two foods, television shows, or other items, and they decide which one they like better. They love to play this, and it helps them become more conscious of their likes and dislikes. Have adolescents make a list of 20 things they like to do in order of preference.

*Challenge unreasonable beliefs held by kids.* The superego sometimes latches onto these ideas and uses them against the ideal self, whereas a healthy superego complements and supports the ideal self. For example, a young girl who shies away from her personal dream of becoming a doctor because "Doctors should be men" can be enlightened and encouraged by you.

Also, never let young people get away with an "I can't" statement. It is a fact that most of us can do anything we put our minds to. Telling ourselves that we can't do something is an unreasonable belief, and it is especially destructive if it closes off options we'd really like to pursue. I used to tell myself, "I'd like to teach, but I just can't speak in front of groups." After forcing myself to address small groups on several occasions, I got over my fear and learned to love public speaking. If we believe we can't do something, then we in fact can't; it is far more honest to say "I won't" than "I can't."

*Encourage young people to think about God.* The issue

of spiritual formation is too complex to go into very much here. Certainly, different adults enjoy different privileges with young people in this regard; parents and ministers, in particular, enjoy a privileged place in the spiritual lives of young people. Nonetheless, it is appropriate for any significant adult at least to ask young people from time to time what they believe about God and the meaning of life. Remember, spirituality is critical to the survival of the ego-ideal in adulthood. Consider this passage written by psychologist Carl Jung:

> During the past thirty years, people from all civilized countries on the earth have consulted me. Among all my patients in the second half of life — that is to say, over thirty-five — there has not been one whose problem in the last resort was not that of finding a religious outlook on life. It is safe to say that every one of them fell ill because he had lost that which the living religions of every age have given to their followers, and none of them has been really healed who did not regain his religious outlook.

People who shoot for anything less than the spiritual stars seem destined to grow flat and disillusioned through the years.

*Allow young people different experiences of people, cultures, beliefs, and lifestyles.* Do this through books, magazines, movies, guest speakers, and travel. Give them food for their dreams, but help them process all this data.

*Share your own dreams with young people.* Maybe you have learned in this chapter the sad truth that your own dream self is not as vital as it could be. Share even this with young people. It might help them appreciate the value of their own dreams.

People who are in the process of growing into their dream selves will not suffer very often from boredom and apathy. They will have a clear idea of who they are and who they want to become, so they will not find it too difficult to settle on a particular type of occupation. They will also develop recreational habits appropriate for their personal talents, and they will not overly regret their limitations. Of course, they may go through periods of struggle and confusion as their dream selves are transformed into ever-new personal ideals and challenges, but even then they will remain hopeful and alive. "Those who believe in the future live in it today," wrote Ayn Rand. Without dreams, "most men lead lives of quiet desperation," wrote Henry David Thoreau. Let us help young people avoid Thoreau's nightmare and at the same time discover deep, personal meaning for their lives.

## Questions for Reflection and Discussion

1. Why is it important for young people to be able to set goals for their lives?
2. What are your own personal dreams for the future? How have your dreams changed through the years?
3. How are you helping young people develop and work toward their own personal dreams?
4. Why is spirituality such an important part of shaping a personal dream?

# 6

# Dealing with Feelings

The movie *Star Trek: The Motion Picture* from 1979 had a most revealing message. Sent to combat a universal menace that was systematically destroying solar systems, the crew aboard the Starship *Enterprise* found themselves matching wits with an ancient earth satellite. The *Voyager* probe, originally programmed to accumulate "all possible knowledge" as it ventured through our solar system beginning in the 1970s, had continued feeding itself the knowledge of the universe for centuries thereafter. But it had reached a critical threshold when it realized that something more than mere knowledge was needed to help make sense of the universe. Ironically, it was the logical Mr. Spock who discovered that the missing element was feelings.

What are feelings? How important are they? Why don't we just ignore them and, like Mr. Spock, live acording to the dictates of pure, impersonal logic? This chapter will attempt to respond to these questions and discuss ways in which we can help young people learn to express feelings appropriately.

## Feelings and Meaning

Feelings play a very special role in the human psyche. By simply observing our most common responses to statements about feelings expressed by others, we can begin to appreciate what feelings tell us about ourselves. For example, what is the first word that comes to mind when people tell you they are angry or sad or happy? Surely you want to ask, "Why?" But when we ask this question, we are not after the kind of knowledge sought by physical scientists. Why people become happy, sad, or angry cannot always be explained in the technical language of hormones and other biochemicals. Our inquiries into the sources of feelings put us in touch with curiosity about the meaning of life, which is one of our most human characteristics.

Feelings tell us the meaning of the events in our lives. They are, in a sense, spiritual barometers, revealing to us the meaning of our values and our perceptions about the world. Pleasant feelings move us into deeper involvements with people, things, and circumstances that are presumably good for us; unpleasant feelings do the opposite. The quality of our life experiences can thus be evaluated by noting the way we feel, which in turn tells us much about our attitudes. Feelings provide information that logic, with its emphasis on the "whatness" of things, neglects.

**Feelings and Attitudes**

We have all seen at some time or another how two different people can experience entirely different feelings in response to the same circumstances. A classical proverb has it that a cup can be half-empty or half-full, depending on how you look at it. One person will lament getting older because of the loss of youthful beauty; another will rejoice in the maturity and grace that comes with passing years. The truth of the matter is that it is not so much what happens to us that stimulates our feelings, but how we *interpret* what happens. That is where the question of meaning comes in.

Many people believe that external circumstances determine their inner emotional states. How many times have we heard someone say, "She makes me so mad"? Such people allow themselves to feel good when good things happen and bad when bad things happen. What a blatant admission of powerlessness this is! Small wonder that so many young people turn to external stimuli like alcohol, drugs, food, and television to stimulate their feelings.

One of the first things we need to teach young people is that they are responsible for their own feelings. No one can deny that external stimuli ("She called me a bad name!") provoke certain automatic responses, but attitudes play a critical role in filtering the perceptions that generate feelings. Calling someone a bad name before his friends will probably always hurt, but there are things the injured party can do even in the heat of the moment to reinterpret the situation without denying its severity.

It will not be easy to help young people own up to their feelings. As babies they were truly powerless over their environment and so were completely dependent on their parents to create pleasant circumstances for them. Through the years, however, they should have learned to be less dependent on their parents and more capable of creating their own circumstances for happiness. Unfortunately, many parents deprive their children of the opportunity to make decisions for themselves; when schools and other institutions follow suit, kids get the message that they are unable to do anything to make themselves happy. So they wait for us to entertain them, saying, "There's nothing to do around here!" Even so, it is possible to help young people realize that there are plenty of ways they can create happy circumstances for themselves without relying on parents or the community to help them.

## Forming Healthy Attitudes

A person's attitude is his or her subjective stance toward the world. This personal stance is determined by one's own self-perceptions, knowledge, and values. We have already discussed ways in which we can help young people develop positive self-perceptions and clarify their values, but it is important, too, to affirm the role of education in helping them attain a healthy understanding of reality. Ignorance does breed misunderstanding and irresponsible behavior.

As adults working with young people, it is our responsibility to help them experience a maximum of pleasant feelings in the real world while learning to cope with unpleasant feelings. We do not want them to withdraw into a fantasy world, but to live with their eyes wide open, enjoying life as much as possible. To do this, they will need healthy attitudes. Listed below are a few ways we can help them grow in this area.

*Explore with young people the attitudes that reinforce their feelings.* It's hard to change an attitude unless one becomes conscious of it. Perhaps the journal approach outlined in Activity 5 can be helpful here.

I used to get angry with my wife because she would not cook breakfast for me. When I finally looked at the attitudes underneath these feelings, I discovered that my expectations were subconscious projections based on the way my mother had treated my father. My mother always made breakfast for my father, therefore my subconscious concluded that good wives fix breakfast for their husbands. Until I realized this, however, I had no way to change my feelings about the situation.

*Affirm healthy attitudes when you find them.* Help young people understand why certain attitudes promote health while others endanger health. For example, I often ask young people to write down three reasons why they should not use drugs. When reading their answers back, I comment positively on those that make good sense.

*Challenge unreasonable beliefs* that make up poor attitudes. For example:

1. People must not make mistakes.
2. If people knew the real me, they would not like me.
3. I'm the only one in the world who feels this way.
4. Everyone must always like me.
5. Physical appearance is the most important thing about a person.
6. Winning is all that matters.
7. It's OK to break rules as long as you don't get caught.
8. Whites are better than nonwhites.
9. Males are better than females.
10. It's not OK to feel angry at my parents from time to time.
11. I am responsible for the way my parents feel.
12. Being rich is the key to happiness.
13. There is no future to hope in.

These are all attitudes that spawn unhealthy behaviors and negative feelings; they must be changed. Unfortunately, these attitudes are quite common among young people today.

In the breakfast incident mentioned above, I had to challenge the unreasonable belief that good wives always fix breakfast for their husbands. After acknowledging to myself that Lisa is a good wife even when she does not fix breakfast, and after hearing her say that she did not care to make a commitment to fix breakfast every day, I was in a position to restructure my expectations. As things stand, our schedules don't always match, so I am responsible for fixing my own breakfast. On the occasions when she does manage to cook for me, my response is gratitude. Changing my attitude in this situation by replacing my unreasonable beliefs with realistic expectations enabled me to move away from anger toward gratitude.

*Encourage young people to consider religious truths concerning the meaning of life* and to form their perspectives around these truths. Their attitudes about death, uniqueness, and the future can receive injections of hope and courage from religious teachings.

*Encourage and support young people in developing positive attitudes about themselves and life.* If you are in a school setting, consider using some of the curricular materials listed at the back of this book. Young people can also benefit from reading and discussing with you one or more of the books from the suggested reading list also at the back of this book. Coaches can work positive attitude messages into chats with their teams, improving their players' performances in the process.

*Take a look at your own attitudes and how they affect your feelings.* Share your own insights in this area with young people. The human brain is more glorious than any computer we will ever devise, but it is up to us to program it properly. That's what forming healthy attitudes is all about.

## Expressing Feelings

It would be wonderful if we could form healthy attitudes so thoroughly that all unpleasant feelings would be completely eliminated from our lives. But most of us will never attain this level of saintliness, and certainly the young people we work with are not there yet. We must therefore learn how to express our feelings—even the most discomfiting ones—in ways that are at least harmless.

Feelings are energy. They are the living connections between people in relationships. If feelings are absent, relationships are practically dead and meaningless. Because of the energy stored in feelings, many people are afraid of them (especially anger); they don't want to lose control. But once the energy of feeling has been released within us, this energy must be expressed. This fact bears repeating: *emotional energy must eventually be expressed.* There are four ways we do this:

*Repression*—ignoring, denying, or deliberately squelching certain feelings, usually anger and fear. If this continues for too long, one becomes emotionally numb or discharges this energy through ulcers, compulsive behaviors, or heart ailments. Research indicates that constant repression can even cause cancer.

*Acting out*—letting the feeling take control of you and behaving according to its impulses (for example, yelling and fighting when angry). One's sense of reason assumes a secondary role in these situations.

*Indirect report*—owning up to your feelings, but explaining them away by making judgments about external events and circumstances that provoked them. For example, "I'm mad because you're such a lazy person" or even a positive judgment such as "I'm happy because you're so good."

*Direct report*—owning up to your feelings and attitudes and saying so by using I-messages ("I feel ____________ when/because ____________"). Note here the separation between one's feelings and the issue at hand.

Of these four ways to express feelings, only direct report is consistantly healthy, and only indirect report is always unhealthy. Contrary to popular belief, it is sometimes very healthy to act out feelings; jog away your anger, for example, or surrender to the joy of a beautiful sunset. It is also healthy at times to repress feelings, such as when expressing mild annoyances would produce unnecessary turmoil. In such cases, it is necessary to talk, write, or exercise away frustrations later on.

**Feelings and Consequences**

Let us consider briefly the consequences that go with the different ways we express feelings. The situation: Mrs. Jones is angry because her son Mike left the car lights on overnight and killed the battery, leaving her without transportation when she is already running late for work.

*Repression* might leave her feeling cold and angry toward her son, who would in turn be confused and possibly even hurt by his mother's stony silence and icy glances. She may be able to work through some of her anger during the day, realizing that Mike is only human and that he did not really mean to kill the car battery. If she does not come to this realization, her repressed anger will hurt her physical health and lead to a temporary distancing between herself and her son.

*Acting out* in this case can only spell trouble. Yelling and screaming would help Mrs. Jones discharge her anger, but she would later have to deal with her unpleasant feelings of guilt for pouncing on Mike. He, in turn, would grow defensive and might even reply with a few choice words of his own. Acting out could only widen the rift in their relationship and would do nothing to fix the car battery or get Mrs. Jones to work.

*An indirect report* would find Mrs. Jones saying that she is angry because her son is so forgetful and irresponsible. He would sooner disappear than hear these shaming remarks. A person receiving this kind of message will probably become angry and defensive and will know little about why his behavior provoked anger. Indirect reports can also express positive sentiments. For example, "I'm glad because you're so nice" is generally affirming. But it would be more helpful for a young person to be told that you thought what he did was nice.

*A direct report* using I-messages would enable her to express her anger and tie it to the real issue: the dead battery and the lost transportation on this hurried morning. Mike, whose self-concept would be left intact, could more easily own up to his mistake, apologize, and help her resolve the transportation problem. In such tight spots, two heads are better than one.

Only the direct report allows Mrs. Jones to do what she really needs to do: express her anger and begin trying to figure out a way to get to work. It leaves her feeling respectful of her son and keeps him from feeling rejected because he made a mistake. Every other mode of expressing anger would leave the two more distant and estranged. And for what? A lousy car battery!

To be sure, we all love our spouses and young people more than we love car batteries, clean rooms, sharpened pencils, tidy clothing, and the many other items we often yell about. But because we are usually so inept at expressing our own feelings in healthy ways, our love often gets lost in counter-messages of repression, acting out, and judgment. We often shame the very people we are trying to help because we have not yet learned to give I-messages or to repress slight annoyances and deal with them later.

## Guidelines for Helping Young People

*Examine your own modeling* to see how you express feelings, especially anger.

*Help young people learn to identify their feelings.* Occasionally ask them how they feel. Invite them to share with you times when they feel sad, glad, mad, or afraid. Use feeling lists (see Activity 6) to help them expand their feeling vocabulary and emotional awareness.

*Teach young people to give I-messages.* If you can substitute the words *I think* for *I feel* in a statement, it is not an I-message. Use examples such as those on the Feelings Expression Worksheet (Activity 7) to help young people differentiate between I-messages and other modes of expression.

*Explore with young people times when it is appropriate to repress or act out feelings.* Give them examples of when and how to do so. In the case of repression, explore ways of getting pent-up feelings out of your system later (talking to a someone, writing in a journal, jogging, meditating, etc.).

**Special Problems**

Shame-based kids, especially those with substance-abusing parents, may have a difficult time getting in touch with their feelings, much less expressing them appropriately. They often act out through humor, over-achieve, or behave irresponsibly to discharge their feelings, but these are only defenses of sorts. Living in an emotionally turbulent home causes them to build subconscious defense mechanisms to reduce their emotional pain. Unfortunately, these defenses also limit their pleasant experiences as well.

While it is important that these emotionally numb kids eventually learn to identify their feelings and express them appropriately, do not rush them. Their defenses, after all, do serve a useful function in their lives; to lead them too quickly into emotional vulnerability might cause them unnecessary pain. Persevere in your efforts to help them as outlined in this chapter, especially with regard to changing their attitudes, but be very gentle when inviting them to share their feelings.

**Questions for Reflection and Discussion**

1. How do our attitudes shape our feelings?
2. How do you usually express anger?
3. What kinds of unreasonable beliefs do you find young people harboring about themselves and about life? How do you challenge these beliefs?
4. Give some examples of acting-out behaviors.

## ACTIVITY 5

### Feelings and Attitudes Worksheet

For each day or period under consideration, reflect upon key events by examining your behavior, thinking, and feeling patterns. How can you prepare yourself for similar events in the future?

| What happened? | What did you do? | How did you feel? | What were you thinking? | Attitude changes |
| --- | --- | --- | --- | --- |
|  |  |  |  |  |

## ACTIVITY 6

### Basic Feelings List

*Mad*

aggravated
angry
annoyed
furious
indignant
ired
provoked

*Energetic*

alert
alive
enthusiastic
excited
inspired
optimistic
peppy
spunky

*Self-Worth*

affirmed
important
needed
proud
worthy

*Sad*

bad
depressed
disappointed
discouraged
dismal
gloomy
miserable
sorry
sullen
unhappy

*Anxious*

alarmed
bothered
concerned
disturbed
moody
nervous
tense
troubled

*Confusion*

baffled
disorganized

*Glad*

cheerful
delighted
gay
happy

*Scared*

afraid
apprehensive
dreading
fearful
frightened
horrified
terrified

*Guilt*

ashamed
embarrassed
humiliated
regretful
remorse
shameful

*Lonely*

rejected
unloved

(Adapted from list by Hazelden, Box 11, Center City, MN 55012.)

## ACTIVITY 7

### Feelings Expression Worksheet for Groups

Indentify the type of expressions described below as repressing, acting out, indirect report, or direct report. For those that are not direct reports, write in the third column an example of how this expression could be stated as a direct report.

| Expression | Type of Expression | Rephrased as Direct Report |
|---|---|---|
| 1. "This is the worst workshop I've ever been to; the chairs are hard and the materials are irrelevant." | | |
| 2. "Shut up!" | | |
| 3. "I feel foolish coming to you for such a small favor when you're so busy." | | |
| 4. "You must really think you're a big-shot —using all those high-powered words around us!" | | |
| 5. "Clean your room or else I'll beat the tar out of you!" | | |
| 6. Ignoring your | | |

spouse's comment that you are lazy and irresponsible for coming in late, but fuming to yourself.

7. "The food in this restaurant is the worst I've had in ages."

8. "The food in this restaurant is the best I've had in ages."

9. "I'm sad because the picnic we were planning has been rained out."

10. Remaining quiet about a friend's habit of telling racist jokes that offend you; not wanting to anger her.

11. "I'm happy because you're such a wonderful person."

12. "I'm unhappy because you're such a louse!"

13. Spanking a child because he has angered you by spilling a glass of milk at the table.

14. "I'm glad it's Friday."

*Key to Responses*

1. Indirect report. Change to "I am miserable at this workshop because the chairs are hard and the materials seem irrelevant to me."
2. Acting out. Change to "Your noise is bothering me. Could you please be quieter?"
3. Direct report.
4. Indirect report. Change to "I feel confused when you use words I don't understand."
5. Acting out. Change to "I feel angry because you have not cleaned your room."
6. Repressing. Change to "I feel hurt and angry when you call me lazy and irresponsible."
7. Indirect report. Change to "I don't like the food in this restaurant."
8. Indirect report. Change to "I like the food in this restaurant."
9. Direct report.
10. Repressing. Change to "I feel offended when you tell jokes that put other people down."
11. Indirect report. Change to "I enjoy being around you because . . . (list specific behaviors)."
12. Indirect report. Change to "I feel unhappy and disheveled when I come into your home and see all this clutter."
13. Acting out. Change to "I feel aggravated because you spilled your milk."
14. Direct report.

7

# Making Decisions

Those of us who work with young people should have as our goal the nurturing of their character in such a manner that they finally behave responsibly for their own sake, not for ours. We want them to be good and to do good not so much because it pleases us (although this might be important early on), but because they themselves want to do so. Helping young people grow into this level of maturity will require that we work with them on their attitudes, expressions of feelings, and hopes for the future. But there is an additional step they must take, and that is making decisions for themselves. Decision-making enables young people to internalize everything we've talked about so far.

In order to appreciate the critical role of decisions in our lives, it might be helpful to briefly consider this formula:

Behavior = Perceptions + Attitudes + Feelings + Decisions

This represents an adaptation of several schools of behavior and demonstrates the critical role of decisions in our lives. Unlike the old stimulus-response models, which classified behavior as being almost completely determined by environmental cues, this model emphasizes more subjective, internal dynamics. And rightly so. What the above formula proposes is that it is not so much the environment that determines our behavior, but what we perceive the environment to be telling us, what we think and feel about these perceptions, and, finally, what we decide to do. For most of us, this model of behavior rings true, giving an appropriate role to human freedom and responsibility.

### Acting and Reacting

Young people with healthy attitudes frequently behave in ways that are totally incongruent with their hopes for the future and their love of life. Alcohol/drug abuse, sexual irresponsibility, classroom disturbances, and even criminal activity among kids cannot always be explained away as the result of low self-worth or an oppressive environment. In fact, many of the irresponsible acts committed by kids are unplanned and unforeseen. Most occur as a spur-of-the-moment response to peer pressure and impulsiveness. After things die down a bit, these young people are often just as shocked as their parents to comtemplate what they've done.

When young people (or anyone, for that matter) behave impulsively because of peer pressure or strong feelings, the behavioral formula presented above gets short-circuited and converted to this:

Behavior = Perceptions + Feelings

When we remove the important role of attitudes and decision-making from behavioral dynamics, we become reactive animals instead of creators of our own destiny. We allow people and circumstances in the enviornment to "pull our strings," prompting a response determined by superego influence or subconscious feelings. More often than not, this kind of behavior gets us in trouble. I can personally attest to the fact that some of the stupidest things I've ever done happened to me precisely because I abandoned my values and allowed circumstances to make decisions for me. Young people who are pressured into smoking pot or riding in a car with a drunk driver often behave according to the reactive formula above.

As might be expected, young people with positive attitudes react in healthier ways than do kids with low self-worth. But the probability and predictability of responsible behavior increases further if they learn to act—to make conscious decisions—instead of merely reacting to the situation at hand. Healthy and dependent kids who begin to make decisions for themselves will become healthier and less dependent; kids who simply react to the events in their lives will eventually make tragic mistakes. One of our tasks in habilitating young people, then, is to make certain that they learn to use decision-making skills in some of life's more serious matters.

**The Decision-Making Process**

Making decisions involves several steps which the human mind seems very naturally disposed to pursue.

*Identify the issues at hand and phrase them as questions.* Let us suppose, for example, that 17-year-old Melissa is facing a situation where her date has gotten drunk. This common occurrence raises not one, but many issues for her: What will her friends think? Will he make sexual advances? Should she ever see him again? For our purposes, let us deal with only one important issue: Should she ride back with him, and if not, what should she do?

*Examine alternatives.* Melissa might consider offering to drive, asking a friend to drive, going home with a friend, or calling her parents. She also might decide to risk the ride with her date.

*List pros and cons for each alternative.* Obviously, her relationship with the young man and her own self-worth figure heavily in these considerations. The pros and cons will be determined for the most part by her self-worth, knowledge of the situation, and values. It is my belief that many young people are turning away from marijuana not because they have healthier self-concepts,,but because they have learned a few things about the harmfulness of pot that count as cons in the decision to smoke or not. We hope that Melissa will know a little about the dangers of riding with a drunk driver.

*Pursue the highest priority alternative.* Our values help us set priorities. If Melissa feels that preserving her relationship with her date is the most important consideration, she will probably choose to stick out the evening with him and hope for the best. If she believes that getting herself home safely is most important, she might offer to drive; failing that, she might go on to other alternatives, calling her parents if all else fails.

This is a relatively uncomplicated process, but one that is too often ignored. Many people have commented on its structural resemblance to logic and mathematics, and they are correct. Courses in mathematics such as algebra, geometry and trigonometry may never be put to practical use, but they nonetheless discipline the mind to question, set priorities, and make decisions.

## Rehearsing Decisions

Unfortunately, life does not always give us the luxury of time and resources to amble through the decision-making process. We might be able to think this process through when trying to make a career decision, for example, but Melissa in the example above has to make choices about her evening without benefit of a reflection journal, a counselor, or maybe even a friend. Life sometimes requires us to act quickly, and we'd best be prepared for those times.

People who have not thought about issues that may confront them out of the blue will probably react emotionally as the whim of the moment dictates. On the other hand, it is entirely possible for people to act quickly and decisively if they have previously thought about the issues at hand and formulated for themselves personal policies about these issues. How easy it would be for Melissa if she had already anticipated this moment beforehand and formulated for herself a clear, unambiguous personal policy to invoke when she'd face it. She might say, "I'm very sorry, but I don't ride with drunk drivers," feeling supported by the thinking she'd already put into this issue.

Young people need adults to help them identify and make decisions about issues that life might present suddenly and without warning. It is especially important to raise and work through the issues listed below, for mistakes in any of these areas could be devastating. (Activity 8 is a worksheet that allows young people to express their feelings on these issues in writing.)

1. Will you ride in a car with a drunk driver?
2. Will you drink alcohol at parties? If so, will you tell your parents about your decision?
3. If you decide to drink, what will your limit be? Will you drive after drinking?
4. Will you smoke marijuana?
5. Will you smoke cigarettes?
6. Will you try to date many people, or will you try to go steady with someone?
7. Will you have sex before marriage?
8. If you decide to remain a virgin until marriage, then what will be your limits for physical affection in the meantime?

9. If you decide to have sex with someone, are you ready for the possibility of conceiving a child? If not, what preventive measures will you take?
10. Will you pick up hitchhikers?
11. How will you respond if someone insults you or picks a fight with you?

There are, of course, many additional life issues that could be listed. For example, young people will eventually have to decide if they will finish high school, if they will go to college, and what kind of career they will pursue. They will seldom have to make snap decisions about these issues, however. The 11 issues listed above are different in that they often confront kids unexpectedly and in a context of peer pressure; they also have serious health implications. This is why we need to work with young people to prepare them to face these issues in a responsible manner.

In addition to using the worksheet approach, we can help young people rehearse their responses to tight spots by using brainstorming, group discussions, role-playing, one-on-one chats, discussions after relevant films and television programs, and short essays. Values clarification and decision-making curricular materials are available through most education departments, providing helpful tools and exercises for the classroom. Finally, your own personal sharing concerning important life issues can be a powerful source of guidance to young people.

### Refusal Skills

Even after helping young people formulate firm personal policies, there is no guarantee that they will be able to stave off peer pressure. Peer pressure is an awesome force, as we adults know from our own adolescent years and even recent experiences. Many a strong, independent person has buckled during a vulnerable moment to appease friends or just to avoid a hassle. That is why we must further strengthen our young people by helping them not only to assert their own personal choices, but also to refuse to compromise themselves.

Many professionals in the health field have begun to point out the importance of teaching kids to say no. Rehearsing these strategies with them ahead of time can provide them with different ways to express their policies when they find themselves under pressure. Brainstorming ways to say no with them will probably tap their own wisdom in this area, many of which are summarized below:

*Direct statements.* "No." "No, thank you; I'd rather not." Few peers will challenge this kind of refusal.

*Broken record.* Keep repeating direct statements. It takes an awfully pushy person to break through this strategy.

*Excuses.* "I can't; I have to stay with my little brother." "My parents are expecting me soon." This provides a less controversial way out.

*Life-goal conflict statements.* "Sorry, I'm in training." "This could mess up my career."

*Personal values statements.* "No, thanks. This goes against my religious beliefs." "I love my body and don't want to hurt myself."

*Statements about consequences.* "I've seen what can happen to people who do that; it's a risk I don't want to take."

*Walking away.* Simply get away from the situation.

These skills can be used in combination, of course, depending on the severity of the situation. Practice them with your kids. Role-play situations where they might be used, and let the participants share how it felt to give and receive refusal statements.

**Supporting Kids' Decisions**

If young people had to make only one decision about sex, drugs, alcohol, and fighting, their lives would be much safer and our responsibilities to them much simpler. This is not the case, however. They will have to make decisions about these and other important health issues many times during their lives.

Because there are so many unhealthy influences in our society, we need to keep in mind the fact that staying healthy and growing up to be mature, responsible adults is an ongoing struggle for young people. This is why we must continually affirm them, encourage them to hope and dream, discipline them, and support them in the decisions they've made for themselves. We cannot give them an attitude/decision vaccine and be done with it, nor can we talk about important health issues only once every few months (and then only in a superficial way).

Many schools and churches are now providing support groups in which young people can meet and discuss critical health issues. I can personally attest to the effectiveness of these groups, since I have seen young people who participate grow healthier and more confident because of them. The best situation is for groups to meet during school time; it's hard for an activity like this to compete with other after-school distractions. Young people are allowed to leave class, provided they make up whatever they miss while in group. School administrators who allow young people with problems to meet with an adult group leader are doing something positive to help dependent kids become more successful in school. We need these groups for young people of all ages.

Teachers might also find it beneficial to have students share in oral and written form about difficult decisions they have had to make. Such exercises take only a few minutes of classtime and provide a unique opportunity for educators to learn more about what's happening with young people. Affirming their healthy decisions and talking more with them about difficult issues can help them tremendously.

Parents, coaches, and ministers also have many opportunities to talk personally with young people about what's going on with them. Be sure to affirm their healthy decisions, even though they made them for their own good and not just to please you. One of my sisters recently made a decision to move out of a dorm room she was sharing with a young woman who turned out to be a pot-smoking party enthusiast. I was pleased that my father phoned her and shared how proud he was of her. Those kinds of decisions can leave young people feeling quite lonely; our support can lessen their self-doubt and help to brace them for future struggles.

It is also worth mentioning at this point the encouraging fact that most of our young people are still making healthy decisions most of the time. There is something to be said for positive peer pressure. If "everybody" is not getting stoned or bed-hopping but trying to keep themselves straight and growing instead, we need to say so from time to time. High schoolers are notorious liars concerning their sexual exploits and alcohol and drug experiences, but these exaggerations often lead younger kids to believe that sex and alcohol and drug use are normal teenage behaviors. Find a group of healthy teenagers and work with them until they feel comfortable going into elementary schools to talk to younger students. These peer educators can help younger kids begin to see that health is what we should consider normal and that true "coolness" comes from the effort to be happy, healthy, and drug-free.

**Questions for Reflection and Discussion**

1. Do you agree that behavior is the result of combining perceptions, attitudes, feelings, and decisions? Explain.
2. What is the difference between acting and reacting? Give some examples of both.
3. What kind of major life decision are you struggling with now? How are you working through this issue?
4. Glance over the questions on life issues listed in this chapter. How are you helping young people work through these decisions?

## ACTIVITY 8
### Decision-Making Worksheet

This worksheet can help young people work through the 11 life issues mentioned in this chapter and other issues as well.

| Issue | Consequences if I say "yes" | | Alternative | |
|---|---|---|---|---|
| | Positive | Negative | if I say "no" | My decision |
| *Example:* Will I ride in a car with a drunk driver? | | | | |

## ACTIVITY 9
## Decision-Making in Groups

### Brainstorms

Invite the individuals in a support group to respond to open-ended questions. Write their answers on a blackboard or a large sheet of paper. Do not debate; accept all responses.

*Examples.* Some of the reasons why young people drink alcohol are . . .
Some young people choose not to drink because . . .

### Voting Questions

Ask for a show of hands or some other indication of individuals' positions regarding an issue. This makes an excellent follow-up to brainstorms. Invite selected individuals to explain their decisions.

*Example.* "How many of you have decided you will not drink alcohol? Please raise your hands. Richie, would you mind sharing one of the most important considerations that went into your decision?"

### Small Group Discussions

In groups of 5-7, have the young people arrive at a consensus opinion concerning certain topics. Use a numerical value scale from 1-5 to express disagreement/agreement.

*Example.* Have the group discuss the statement, "Teenagers should not drink alcohol until they reach the legal drinking age." Ask the group member to reach a consensus and express it on a numerical scale between 1 (strongly disagree) and 5 (strongly agree). When the small groups come back together, have a spokesperson for each group share the group's consensus and discuss some of the thinking that went into it.

**Role-Playing**

Role-playing allows students an opportunity to personalize their responses to an issue. Establish clear, specific situations. Afterwards, ask the participants to discuss their feelings for maximum effect, and invite the audience to suggest alternative ways of dealing with the issues. Try the following:

*Examples.* Two friends try to introduce a third to his first marijuana joint, but he tries to refuse.

Two friends try to talk a third into giving them the keys to her car because she is too drunk to drive, and the abuser refuses to hear of it.

Two friends try to counsel a third to stop smoking cigarettes.

8

# Environmental Concerns

During the past twenty years, numerous writers have reported the experiences of those who survived imprisonment in Nazi concentration camps. Life in these prisons was unbelievably harsh, and it is hard for us to understand how so many people could have cooperated in such a hideous venture. The Nazi bureaucracy created an environment that enabled fairly decent individuals to become sadistic and callous. German boys raised by God-fearing parents somehow came to believe that they were doing a very good thing by killing off Jews. How Adolf Hitler used his government to spread and implement this belief is one of the most sobering stories in all of human history.

The relationship between environment and attitude is borne out in the lives of concentration camp survivors. Psychiatrist Viktor Frankl, himself a survivor of Auschwitz and Dachau, pointed out that for many prisoners, having something to live for made the difference between life and death. Camp life quickly reduced even the healthiest of men and women to walking skeletons. Only the human spirit and its will to live enabled many prisoners to remain alive for that extra day, week, or month until liberation came to them.

Many people have read Frankl and other survivors and drawn rose-colored conclusions of their own. Unquestionably, these inspiring men and women are living testimonies to the indomitability of the human spirit. But let us not be too quick to conclude that human attitudes can be adjusted to interpret any oppressive circumstances favorably. Of those who survived the concentration camps, few were left without deep emotional scars.

The work of behaviorists like B. F. Skinner also points out the importance of environment in shaping attitudes and behavior. Behavior modification programs and clinics are being used effectively by schools and counselors to help young poeple change self-destructive behavior.

Because almost everything I have discussed in this book thus far has focused on internal and subjective dynamics such as self-concept, feelings, personal aspirations, and decisions, you might conclude that environmental factors are relatively unimportant. But attitudes are not formed in an existential vacuum. It is theoretically possible for a ghetto child to grow up to be as positive and optimisitc as Dr. Norman Vincent Peale, but realistically the odds of this happening are quite small.

Human needs are attended to and fulfilled in an environment of some kind. Some environmental situations facilitate this process better than others. Because home and school provide the environmental contexts in which most young people grow, this chapter will address concerns related to these areas. Certain external factors at home and at school make habilitation difficult. We must therefore help young people to avoid or cope with the detrimental influences they may be confronting in their everyday lives. We may find, too, that it is necessary for us to work to change those structures and influences when and where we can. One of the greatest gifts we can give our young people is a healthy environment to grow in.

**Alcohol/Drug Availability**

Many studies have shown that the probability of a young person's becoming involved with alcohol and drugs is directly related to the number of times he or she will be faced with opportunities to use them. The strategies I suggest for reducing chemical dependency are very simple. In the case of alcohol, encourage abstinence for as long as possible, then discourage abuse when young people do begin drinking. In the case of drugs, my strategy is even simpler: discourage all recreational drug use. When alcohol and drugs are too easily accessible to young people, our strategies for helping them will be sabotaged. We can encourage them to search for straight friends and chemical-free gatherings, but we also have a civic responsibility to work toward the elimination of illegal drugs from our streets and alcohol sales to minors in our stores and bars.

Are you willing to get involved in the fight to reduce alcohol and drug availability? Will you get together with other adults to sponsor and chaperone alcohol/drug-free gatherings for young people? Have you complained lately about bars and stores that sell alcohol to minors? Will you affirm your police when they make a bust? Too often we blame police for the availability of drugs, then threaten to sue them when our own children are busted.

Many young people get their alcohol from the home. If you become aware of this, will you notify the parents involved? If the parents do not respond, will you notify a child advocate agency? How about becoming personally involved with chemical-using young people and contracting with them to remain abstinent for awhile (see Activity 10)? Better yet, how about starting a support group for young people who need help to stop using alcohol and/or drugs?

**Oppressive Home Environments**

Many young people come from homes marred by the turmoil of divorce, unemployment, and parental alcoholism or drug use. Also, many of our so-called healthy homes evidence several of the characteristics of dysfunctional family situations listed below:

—people protect, deny and repress feelings
—performance is more important than people
—many taboo subjects; lots of secrets
—punishment by shaming
—unclear, inconsistent rules
—anger is most-expressed feeling
—members cannot cope with stress
—members are always tired
—little affirmation
—lots of criticism

Children who grow up in these homes will suffer deep emotional pain. Some will nonetheless be high achievers. Others will be troublemakers, or extremely sensitive, or completely "average." What these children all have in common is an inability to articulate and express their unpleasant feelings. Surviving in turbulent home situations calls for the development of strong defense mechanisms, but behind these lie mountains of loneliness, disappointment, fear, anger, and even guilt (for believing they've caused their parents' difficulties).

Any adult involved with young people will have opportunities to help kids from oppressive home situations. One out of every four kids comes from a home where parental alcohol abuse is a problem. If these young people grow up without help, they will perpetuate the problem, becoming alcoholics themselves and raising children who will also be hurt. We must break this cycle of violence in whatever ways we can (see Activity 11), for we just might be the only knowledgeable and healthy adults involved with certain young people who can do so.

Adults often feel overwhelmed and discouraged when facing the issue of dysfunctional families. "What good can we do against such odds?" they lament. But it is important to remember that all people prefer health to sickness; most young people will eagerly respond to your efforts to strenghten them. Maybe we won't be able to fix things up at home for them, but we can still teach them to cope at home in non-destructive ways and try to live normal and healthy lives away from home. We should not allow their home difficulties to discourage us. Instead, we can teach them another set of survival skills to use in addition to the one they've already learned. They need to learn to survive in a world of health as much as a world of sickness. If they live two different lives—a miserable one at home and a reasonably healthy one away from home —this is still better than constant misery, isn't it?

Child abuse is an issue that we cannot ignore. Abused young people are usually reluctant to own up to parental abuse because of their shame and fear. Let your young people hear that you know some parents abuse their children and that if any of them have this problem, you are willing to discuss it with them in privacy and confidentiality. Many times they do not even know who they can turn to, so identify yourself as a resource to them. Learn what child protection agencies there are in your area, and get additional help from them for abused young people. This is one matter you can't handle alone.

## School Problems

Young people spend the best hours of their days at school. Most teachers do everything in their power to teach what is required in as interesting and stimulating a manner as possible while maintaining classroom discipline. And most principals try to support teachers in these efforts while juggling bus routes, parental complaints, building maintenance, and other problems. But incompetent teachers and principals are not an endangered species. When incompetent educators work with young people, an already bad situation is worsened. School is one of four institutions where people are sent and held against their will (the other three being prison, mental hospitals, and the military during times of conscription). Oversized classes and inadequate materials make teaching difficult even for highly skilled, caring people. Educators who relate poorly to young people and cannot maintain classroom discipline will accomplish very little in the way of habilitating young people.

Even more significant than teacher competency is the quality of the school principal. Those of us who work with schools have a saying: "As goes the principal, so goes the school." Unfortunately, there are many principals who view their schools as private kingdoms. Many were appointed not so much because they have good administrative skills but because they were "in tight" with a few school board members. In such cases, faculty morale is low and parental involvement is usually discouraged. Principals who run their schools as fiefdoms must realize that the young people are the losers.

In a school with healthy principals and teachers, one may note:

—high school spirit, pride, and enthusiasm among students
—highly visible and forceful principal providing leadership
—many curricular choices
—unified faculty with high morale
—principal and teachers know most students by name
—community involvement in school functions
—parents' voluntary involvement in school functions
—clean and well-kept facilities and grounds
—fair and consistent enforcement of school rules
—mechanisms for airing student complaints and grievances.

Our young people deserve nothing less than this. They have only one life to live, and their educational years are too precious to waste. We adults ought to insist on the highest-quality education possible for our children. A few adults at a school board meeting can be a powerful force for change. Sometimes, too, a little money for building improvements and teacher raises can help to boost morale.

Are you willing to join the struggle to help improve our schools? Are you willing to encourage others to join you in evaluating the way principals are running our schools? Can you volunteer to help on campus? Why not offer to help chaperone a social activity, or co-sponsor a school club?

**Television**

Young people today grow up in the noisiest environment in history. The average home is filled with television's influences for over six hours each day. In addition, adolescents listen to radio or stereo music at almost every opportunity. Many researchers are beginning to conclude that we pay a very high price for this inordinate amount of attention to our entertainment machines.

Before launching into a critique of the influences of television, we must first recognize the very positive educational and entertainment possibilities these inventions still do offer. If utilized wisely, they can enrich our lives. In our own homes, we can learn about people and places that our forebears never knew existed. But if we are to make the most of these positive experiences, we must first quit using television as a babysitter or diversion.

I have referred to the government report *Television and Behavior* (1982 DHHS Publication 82-1195) several times in this book. It is the definitive compilation of research on television to date, summarizing over 2,500 research reports accumulated over the past decade. Some of its conclusions were reported in the media, most notably in newspapers; much of it, however, was downplayed. But anyone who reads the report will surely grasp the significance of the following points, especially since television gives young people their primary information about our culture.

*Television and health.* Prime-time characters drink alcohol twice as often as coffee, 14 times as often as soft drinks, and 15 times as often as water. Kids see 10 drinking episodes per day, 3,000 per year. Few consequences are ever shown. Only 2 percent of these characters have drinking problems.

Seventy percent of all food commercials are for foods that are high in fat, cholesterol, sugar, and salt. On Saturday morning television, 67 percent of all commercials are for sweets and other low-nutrition snacks. The nutritional value of a person's diet is inversely related to the amount of television he or she watches.

In addition, prime-time characters seldom wear seat-belts.

On the plus side, only 11 percent of all men and 2 percent of all women on TV smoke. These percentages are lower than the general population and lower than prime-time character percentages from a decade ago. As mentioned in chapter 1, since cigarette advertising was taken off the air in the early 1970s, smoking among teenagers has decreased 50 percent.

*Television and aggressive behavior.* There is an average of 5 violent acts per hour on prime-time shows, 18 on Saturday mornings. The pain and suffering that result from violence are seldom shown. Watching television violence increases aggressive behavior. Children learn that aggressive behavior is an acceptable way to meet their needs. In addition, the more a person sees violence on television, the less responsive he or she becomes to violence in the real world. Still, people who watch lots of television believe the world is more dangerous than do people who don't watch very often.

*Television and attitudinal development.* Once a person gets used to televised sex and violence, more explicit acts are required to arouse the same response. Preschoolers have a hard time understanding sarcasm and discriminating between real and fantasy violence.

In other studies involving young children, it was found that preschoolers who watch lots of television have lower imaginative and creative skills; they remember stories that are read to them better than they do stories they see on TV; and their emotions are more stimulated by TV than their thinking is. This last factor is why advertising geared toward young children is so effective. Elementary-school-aged kids did not seem adversely affected by one or two hours of television watching each day, but longer periods of viewing were correlated with poor school performance.

Besides these considerations, there is the simple fact that time spent watching television could be spend doing something else. Could it be that television keeps us from playing with our children, or visiting friends and relatives as often as we should, or reading books? And all that noise can't help but rob us of peace of mind and the ability to hear our own thoughts.

Several communities throughout the country have participated in experiments calling for the elimination of television watching at home. After a few weeks, participants were asked to share what differences they'd noticed in their families. Almost without exception, family members had grown closer to one another. Everyone felt more peaceful, and young people did better in school. Many of these families decided to leave their sets off permanently; most decided at least to reduce their hours of viewing time.

It is essential that we recognize the influence that television has in shaping the perceptions and, consequently, the attitudes young people have about themselves and our world. This was the conclusion reached in *Television and Behavior,* and we must shout it from the housetops. The report also offered guidelines for responsible viewing in families, a summary of which is offered in Activity 12.

**Socio-Economic Considerations**

There is no denying the negative effects of poverty, ignorance, and unemployment in our homes and communities. Drug availability, crime, dysfunctional family systems, and poor schools are closely related to low socioeconomic status. Television and alcohol and drugs become ways to escape or at least numb the pain and hopelessness of the poor and disadvantaged.

We must be careful when studying such matters, however. As recently as 50 years ago, during the Great Depression, most American families knew worse poverty than do America's poor today. Still, there can be no doubt that majority and minority groups experienced those difficult years differently. When a black man I know was asked how his family had managed to survive the Depression, he replied, "What Depression?" Undaunted, his questioner described the bland and scanty meals, job shortages, and lack of money most people experienced. "That's the way we've always lived," replied my friend.

Theoretically, it is possible for people to be reasonably happy in poor socio-economic circumstances. No one, after all, has it as bad as did the concentration camp prisoners and even our country's settlers. Few people in the United States die of hunger, and opportunities for educational and career pursuits are open to all as never before. Surely poverty is no virtue, but neither is it an insurmountable obstacle on the road to happiness. This is a message we must keep in mind, lest we fall into the trap of believing that more money or a guaranteed income for all will bring magical relief to lower socio-economic groups. Surely the poor do need emergency relief, but the deeper issues surrounding poverty and oppression are more spiritual than materialistic in nature.

Consider the situation among Southern blacks, for example. In the rural areas where I work, blacks score lower than whites on achievement tests again and again. Yet both groups have the same opportunities for enlightenment at school. I believe this phenomenon is related to history, not genetics as some have claimed. American black culture developed in a context of oppressive dependency upon and subservience to whites. Not until recently have blacks been extended full opportunities to enjoy the benefits of American citizenship, and then only grudgingly and with great controversy.

Until this occurred, blacks did not give education a high priority, because educated blacks would probably have been denied any kind of employment that would have allowed them to utilize advanced degree skills. It is therefore unreasonable to expect that blacks will be able to shake their second-class-citizen identity immediately and participate fully in our society; what took over three centuries to develop cannot be undone in less than three decades. All the money in the world can't change the racial bigotry that still exists in our country among whites and blacks and that stands in the way of full equality in our country more than anything else. In the long run, blacks and whites will simply have to learn to relate as equals and learning to do so is a spiritual issue.

Adults need to try to understand the ways in which socio-economic factors influence the attitudes and decisions of young people. We need to challenge the unreasonable beliefs they have picked up from their culture while respecting the importance of their traditions. I was recently invited to speak to the seniors at an all-white rural private school. For some reason, our discussion drifted into a survey of the drugs of preference among whites and blacks in the area. Several of the students began laughing and mouthing racist slurs, using slang that most blacks would find objectionable. For me, the issue of racism at that moment took precedence over the substance abuse material I'd been brought there to discuss.

I invited the students who'd made the remarks to stand up and repeat their comments. None did so. When I asked why they were ashamed to repeat their words, they did not reply. As their teacher squirmed nervously, I then asked them to share with me what they perceived to be the advantages of being white. Several students hesitantly shared a few points, then more began to open up. I listed these advantages on the board, then asked why they applied to whites but not blacks. These students soon realized that the advantages of being white were denied to blacks because our white majority culture has for centuries oppressed blacks. I concluded with a quote from C. S. Lewis: "The Germans mistreated the Jews because they hated them; later, they hated them because they mistreated them." Many whites hate blacks because they remind us of something about ourselves that we loathe. In order to overcome racism, we must teach young people to challenge and transform these subconcious projections.

Socio-economic issues also challenge us to put our citizenship into action. When blatant injustices are ignored, oppression will continue. Hitler knew this. That is how he was able to build concentration camps practically in the backyards of upstanding citizens who were nonetheless silent citizens. You do not have to become a sign-toting radical to promote justice. Sometimes all that is necessary is a letter to an elected official or to the editor of a newspaper. Also, helping young people to overcome racial and other forms of prejudice is a step in the direction of a more just future. In the long run, we all stand to gain much from your efforts in this regard.

**Questions for Reflection and Discussion**

1. What are you doing about alcohol/drug availability in your area?
2. What can you do when you know parents or teachers are abusing children?
3. How do you feel about the negative consequences

young children can experience from watching too much television?

4. How much television should young people be allowed to watch? Do you agree with the guidelines in Activity 12?
5. What do you do when you hear young people making racist or sexist remarks? Do you believe it is important to challenge them?

## ACTIVITY 10

### Behavior Contract

I, ____(name of young person)____, promise that I will ____(state desired behavior)____ for ____(length of time)____.
By keeping this contract, I will be granted the rewards listed below. If I fail to keep this contract, I will notify ____(name of adult)____ within ____(length of time)____ and will accept the consequences listed below.

| Rewards for keeping contract | Disciplinary Consequences |
|---|---|
| | |

____________________
(signature of young person)

____________________ ____________________
(date) (signature of adult)

## ACTIVITY 11
### Working With Children of Alcoholics

Before beginning to work with children of alcoholics, I suggest you go to Al-Anon and Alateen for awhile to understand their approach to helping codependent people. You should also read Claudia Black's *It Will Never Happen to Me* and Robert Ackerman's *Children of Alcoholics* (see reading list at the back of this book).

1. Work with small groups (2-15). It is important that young people hear from others that they are not alone.
2. Educate them with books, pamphlets, films, and filmstrips concerning the illness of chemical dependency and how it affects families. They need to know that their parent is *ill,* not bad.
3. Use exercises that will help them become more aware of their feelings and more comfortable expressing them. Open-ended sentences such as "A time when I felt happy at home was . . ." and "A time when I was afraid of of my parents was . . ." might be extremely effective.
4. Encourage them to try to lead normal and happy lives at home and to detach emotionally from their parent's drinking behavior.
5. Help them change their attitudes about their role in the home. For example, it is unlikely that they are the cause of their parent's drinking.
6. Let them know it's OK to feel anger toward their alcoholic parent at times. It's what they do with the anger that's important.
7. Validate each young person often through affirma-

tion and physical touch.

8. Impress upon the group the necessity of confidentiality. None of us would want private, painful stories about our families made public.

## ACTIVITY 12
### Television Use Guidelines

1. Work for better programming; support groups that seek to reduce explicit sex, violence, and exploitative advertising.
2. Limit children's viewing time. Preschoolers should watch no more than one hour per day (always with an adult present); other children, no more than two hours.
3. Monitor program selection. Do not leave this entirely up to the kids. Since cable programming now brings a variety of specifically adult shows into our homes, this is especially important.
4. Process information from programs with kids. As you watch television with them, call attention to significant happenings; this increases their awareness of what's going on. Explain the meaning of material that might be confusing to children. Encourage them to ask questions if they don't understand what's happening. Help them to apply what they've seen and draw inferences from it. Ask the child, "What just happened?" "Why did this happen?" "What would have happened if . . . ?" Such questions keep their minds as well as their emotions involved.
5. Exhibit critical viewing skills by processing material with other adults in the presence of children.

9

# P.S. Take Care of Yourself

Just a few closing words now to encourage you to hang in there with young people. Although our work with them can be extremely rewarding, it can also be difficult and frustrating. We are often required to give far more than we thought possible, and this can leave us feeling drained and empty. Do not give up, though, for young people need you more than ever before. Learn how to pace yourself and recharge your own spiritual batteries. A few suggestions from a variety of helping professionals follow.

*Learn to recognize your own stress signals.* Insomnia, nail-biting, hair-pulling, indigestion, mental fragmentation, and emotional acting out are all indications that you need to slow down, take stock, and be good to yourself.

*Practice stress management techniques.* Prayer, meditation, jogging, writing in a journal, massage, talking with friends, and adequate sleep all help to discharge stress overloads and create internal peace.

*Be committed to your own professional and personal growth.* Take time off occasionally to attend workshops, lectures, retreats, conferences, and classes. Keep your own feelings/attitudes journal. Read good books.

*Have fun.* In addition to enjoying your involvements with young people more, take some fun time just for you.

When was the last time you went to a movie or enjoyed a nice meal with friends or played games that you like? Cultivate a sense of humor. Schedule time to "waste"—to do whatever you feel like doing.

*Find a support network.* Attempting to go it alone is sheer madness. Get together with others who work with young people over lunch or after work at least every two weeks to share your highs and lows. If you are a parent, join a parent peer group (or start one yourself—see Activity 13). If your extended family is not nearby, call upon friends and neighbors to give you support.

*Don't get discouraged.* There are so many broken kids and so many harmful influences in our culture that it can get anyone down at times. Keep in mind your successes with young people; don't look back at your failures except to learn from them.

According to a well-known parable, two men were walking along a beach after a tremendous storm had passed through, stranding thousands of starfish ashore. One man remarked how sad it was that so many of the fragile creatures would eventually die. The other began throwing starfish back into the ocean.

"What good does it do to throw these starfish back into the sea?" cried the first man. "You will never save them all; there are far too many!"

But the starfish thrower remained undaunted. He picked up another and pitched it into the water, saying, "You are right, of course. I will never save them all. But to that starfish I just threw into the sea I have made all the difference in the world."

The big picture can be very discouraging. If we focus on individuals, however, the picture changes completely. If we do what we can in our own ways, it will make all the difference in the world to the young people we help.

**Questions for Reflection and Discussion**

1. How do you become aware of stress in your life? What do you do to manage stress?
2. What do you do for fun? How do you feel about being good to yourself?
3. Do you ever feel discouraged when working with young people? Why?
4. How do you work through your disappointments in certain young people?

## ACTIVITY 13

### How to Form a Parent Peer Group

*Find out who your children's friends are.* Ask them directly, check the school yearbook, ask people who know your children, or call the school and ask teachers, guidance counselors, or the principal.

*Contact the parents of your children's friends to meet with you.* Introduce yourself, talk about your interest in mutual parenting, and invite them to come to a meeting at your home on a definite date and time.

*Coordinate the initial meeting.* Make formal introductions, but keep the atmosphere informal. Discuss concerns you have about your child that others are likely to share, and invite others to share. Avoid discussing people who aren't present. Exchange names and phone numbers. Decide when and where to meet again.

*Continue meeting.* Try to meet at least once a month for three months, then evaluate your future needs.

*Agree on mutual guidelines.* At future meetings, begin with making decisions on the issues on which one parent should call another parent: suspicions about something seen or heard, rude behavior, presence of chaperones, checkup on rules, firsthand evidence of irresponsible behavior, and other potential problems. Discuss guidelines and decide which ones the group wishes to render mutual support on (curfews, television privileges, smoking and drinking rules, allowances, limits for parties, study times, use of family car, and so on).

# Suggested Reading

Ackerman, Robert. 1984. *Child of alcoholics: A Guide for Educators, Therapists, and Parents.* Learning Publications, P.O. Box 1326, Holmes Beach, FL 33509. An informative and practical guide to understanding the impact of parental alcoholism on children.

Black, Claudia. 1982. *It Will Never Happen to Me.* Medical Administration Corporation Book Department, 1850 High St., Denver, 80218. A highly readable and informative account of the consequences suffered by children of chemically dependent parents. Provides many helpful suggestions for working with these children.

Buscaglia, Leo. 1972. *Love.* Fawcett Book Groups, New York. Dr. Buscaglia's inspiring account of how he came to lead a class on love and what he learned from this experience.

Campbell, David P. 1974. *If You Don't Know Where You're Going, You'll Probably End Up Somewhere Else.* Argus Communications, One DLM Park, Allen, TX 75002. This light-hearted yet practical book is very helpful for clarifying goals, identifying personal strengths, and improving relationships.

Carnegie, Dale. 1936. *How to Win Friends and Influence People*. Pocket Books, New York. A timeless best-seller as useful today as when it first appeared. Reviews the principles that make relationships enjoyable; examples and case histories are most helpful. Simple and down-to-earth.

Dinkmeyer, Don, and McKay, Gary D. 1973. *Raising a Responsible Child: Practical Steps to Successful Family Relationships*. Simon and Schuster, New York. A straightforward presentation of specific strategies which can be used by parents to help meet their own and their children's needs by two of the leading experts in parenting today.

Emotional Health Anonymous. 1975. *Twelve Steps for Everyone . . . Who Really Wants Them*. CompCare Publications, 2415 Annapolis Ln., Minneapolis, MN 55441. Utilizes the Twelve Step approach of self-help groups to help one grow spiritually and become more emotionally balanced. A good tool for spiritual growth support groups.

Frankl, Viktor E. 1955. *The Doctor and the Soul: From Psychotherapy to Logotherapy*. Random House, New York. Dr. Frankl's reflections on his concentration camp experiences and his discussion of the ways in which counselors can help people come to grips with life's meaning. Not always easy reading, but highly provocative.

Ginott, Haim G. 1965. *Between Parent and Child*. Macmillan, New York. A highly readable best-seller providing many helpful guidelines for communication between parents and children. Also provides disciplinary suggestions for dealing with jealousy, bedtime, TV, and other issues.

Glasser, William. 1976. *Positive Addiction.* Harper and Row, New York. One of the few books that examines the dynamics and significance of alternative highs. Suggests natural high possibilities that anyone can enjoy.

Gordon, Thomas. 1975. *P.E.T., Parent Effectiveness Training.* New American Library, New York. An authoritative and comprehensive treatment of parent-child relationships, emphasizing dialogue and clear communications. Takes a rather permissive approach to discipline, however.

Peck, M. Scott. 1978. *The Road Less Traveled.* Simon and Schuster, New York. Written by a psychotherapist, this best-seller discusses the importance of responsibility and spirituality to individual mental health and quality relationships. Good personal growth reading for anyone.

Powell, John, S.J. 1976. *Fully Human, Fully Alive.* Argus Communications, One DLM Park, Allen, TX 75002. Fr. Powell introduces "vision therapy" as a tool for understanding goals and behavior. Includes many practical exercises. Great for individual and group use by adults and adolescents.

St. Romain, Philip. 1984. *Becoming a New Person: Twelve Steps to Christian Growth.* Liguori Publications, One Liguori Dr., Liguori, MO 63057. Uses a Twelve Step approach with practical suggestions to help individuals become less selfish and more loving. A helpful tool for Christian spiritual growth groups.

Spock, Dr. Benjamin and Rothenberg, Dr. Michael. 1985. *Dr. Spock's Baby and Child Care.* E. P. Dutton, New York. The all-time best-selling standard reference for parents. Provides many suggestions for helping parents deal with the day-to-day problems of raising small children, but is of limited value in suggestions for building self-worth and self-discipline.

Wells, Harold C., and Canfield, Jack. 1976. *One Hundred Ways to Enhance Self Concepts in the Classroom.* Prentice-Hall, Englewood Cliffs, NJ. A wide variety of exercises—some simple, some quite involved—to help teachers strengthen students' attitudes. Every teacher should have a copy and use these exercises regularly.

Ziglar, Zig. 1975. *See You at the Top.* Pelican Publishing Co., P.O. Box 189, Gretna, LA 70053. An instructive and inspiring guide to growth in self-esteem and personal success, written by one of America's leading motivational speakers. Good for personal growth reading and as a growth group guide.

## Suggested Curricular Materials

*Project Charlie,* 5701 Normandale Rd., Edina, MN 55424. (612) 925-9706. A K-6 curriculum stressing self-awareness, relationships, peer pressure, decision-making, and drug information. Training available.

*Me/Me:* Drug Prevention Education Program, 400 S. Linwood Ave., Appleton, WI 54911. (414) 735-0114. A K-6 program utilizing materials to help promote self-worth, responsible expression of feelings, and decision-making. A drug information resource is also provided. Training available.

*Children Are People, Inc.,* 1599 Selby Ave., St. Paul, MN 55104. (612) 644-3033. Stresses a community approach to the prevention of chemical dependency. K-6 school curriculum and support group materials encourage development of self-worth, emotional awareness, responsibility, and decision-making. Training available.

*Operation Aware,* 2410 Morris Thomas Rd., Duluth, MN 55811. (218) 722-6923. For grades 5-6. Deals especially with peer pressure issues.

*8:30 Monday Morning:* American Business Men's Research Foundation, Michigan National Tower, Suite

1208, Lansing, MI 48933. For grades 7-12. Emphasizes alcohol education, lifestyles, decision-making, alternatives, and self-esteem. Materials only available; no training required.

*Skills for Living:* Quest, Inc., 2703 N. Main St., Findlay, OH 45840. (419) 424-9693. For grades 9-12. Emphasizes self-concept, feelings, making friends, family-dating-marriage issues, fiscal responsibility, and career planning. Training required.

*I Can:* Zig Ziglar Corporation, 3330 Earhart, Carrollton, TX 75006. (800) 527-0102. For grades 7-12. Emphasizes positive attitudes, self-discipline, citizenship, and relationships. Training available.

*Say "No" to Alcohol/Drug Abuse:* Alcohol and Drug Abuse Prevention Program, Valley Park Pupil Service Center, 2928 College Dr., Baton Rouge, LA 70808. (504) 928-4729. For grades 6-8. Curriculum guide stressing peer pressure issues, media awareness, decision-making, drug information, and alternatives. Available without training for cost of guide.

Printed in the United States
19031LVS00005B/444